ID742963

CALGARY PUBLIC LIBRARY
FEBRUARY 2014

SPICE
TRIP

STEVIE PARLE & EMMA GRAZETTE

◨ SQUARE PEG
LONDON

Published by Square Peg 2012

10 9 8 7 6 5 4 3 2 1

This book is published to accompany the television series entitled *Spice Trip*, first broadcast on More 4 and Channel 4.

The series was produced by Alchemy TV. Alchemy TV was set up in 2011 by award-winning executive producer Nicola Gooch and entrepreneur Charlie Parsons. The idea for *Spice Trip* was inspired by a visit to a plantation in Kerala.

Copyright © Emma Grazette & Stevie Parle

The Authors have asserted their rights under the Copyright, Designs and Patents Act 1988 to be identified as the authors of this work

Photography © Jason Lowe & Joe Woodhouse
Illustrations © Andrea Joseph

This book is sold subject to the condition that it shall not, by way of trade or otherwise, be lent, resold, hired out, or otherwise circulated without the publisher's prior consent in any form of binding or cover other than that in which it is published and without a similar condition, including this condition, being imposed on the subsequent purchaser

The Random House Group Limited Reg. No. 954009

Addresses for companies within The Random House Group Limited can be found at: www.randomhouse.co.uk

A CIP catalogue record for this book is available from the British Library

ISBN 978 0 22 409572 3

The farms visited for this book and series are ethical estates which do not use child labour and pay a fair wage to employees.

The authors and publisher disclaim, as far as the law allows, any liability arising directly or indirectly from the use, or misuse, of the information contained in this book. The information in this book has been compiled by way of general guidance in relation to the specific subjects addressed, but it is not a substitute and not to be relied on for medical, healthcare, pharmaceutical or other professional advice on specific circumstances and in specific locations. So far as the author is aware the information given is correct and up to date as at October 2012. Practice, laws and regulations all change, and the reader should obtain up to date professional advice on any such issues.

Essential oils are highly concentrated and very potent, so avoid using when pregnant and never use on children. Always dilute the oil in a carrier oil like olive oil, grapeseed or almond oil and never apply pure undiluted oil directly to skin.

Further information on the advice given in this book can be obtained from the National Institute of Medical Herbalists.

The Random House Group Limited supports the Forest Stewardship Council (FSC®), the leading international forest certification organisation. Our books carrying the FSC® label are printed on FSC®-certified paper. FSC® is the only forest certification scheme endorsed by the leading environmental organisations, including Greenpeace. Our paper procurement policy can be found at www.randomhouse.co.uk/environment

MIX
Paper from responsible sources
FSC™ C004592

Food and location photography (except Zanzibar): Jason Lowe
Zanzibar location photography: Joe Woodhouse
Design: Smith & Gilmour
Illustration: Andrea Joseph
Home economist: Annie Nichols
Prop stylist: Cynthia Inions
Herbal consultant: Dee Atkinson
Copy editor: Jan Bowmer

Printed and bound in Wemding, Germany by Firmengruppe APPL

CONTENTS

....

STEVIE

I love to cook with spices and wanted to know more about my favourite ones. I embarked on this mad *Spice Trip* adventure with Emma to get to the very heart of the six spices I consider the most important: cloves, cinnamon, nutmeg, black pepper, chillies and cumin. These are the bedrocks of the spice cupboard, and form the basis of hundreds of recipes from all over the world.

Spices add something so brilliant to food that cooking with them feels naughty, almost like cheating. A scattering of chilli flakes, scratch of nutmeg or a pinch of cumin, can transform the most ordinary ingredients into exciting, vibrant, extraordinary dishes. Most of us have these six spices in our cupboards or in our kitchen and yet we know so little about them.

The most exciting thing about this trip for me was to learn how to cook with each spice from the world's greatest experts – the people who grow, process, sell and cook with them every day. It's been amazing to see the beautiful places that everyday spices like black pepper come from. We use pepper so much we barely think of it as a spice and never give any thought to its history or journey. To think that spices come from some of the most beautiful places on earth is pretty inspiring. At the very least this book should make you stop and take another look at what you are sprinkling on your food, persuade you to throw away the pre-ground, stale old spices lingering in your cupboard and to appreciate spices for the beautiful, delicious, exotic magic seeds that they are.

I found each spice to be truly representative of where they come from. Grenadian people are proud, strong and sexy, like nutmeg; Mexicans, wild, joyous and noisy like chillies; Turkish people calm, proud and exotic like cumin… you get the picture. I honestly won't be able to smell a spice without remembering the extraordinary people we met on our spice trip. It really adds another dimension to food when you can remember the people and imagine the places where the things you eat come from. It's all part of respecting what you eat and enjoying it more fully. It's something I always try to do in my cooking, to communicate a sense of time and place, a connection to where food comes from and a nod to the people who grow and cook it.

The food I love most is simple, fast and homely. It's the food I cook at home and the food I cook in my restaurant, Dock Kitchen. I'm not too interested in things that take hours to prepare, I prefer 'proper' food cooked in people's homes, the food of the grandmothers and great-grandmothers of this world. Food cooked with love, for people you love. So we have jammed this book with recipes that are exciting and easy to make, most of them taking less than 20 minutes to prepare and not much longer to cook so they're ideal for everyday cooking. If you find yourself getting lost, refer to our Cook's notes at the end of the book and they should point you in the right direction.

We chose these recipes to highlight each of the six spices and the different techniques and diverse ways they are used around the world, from British oxtail stew flavoured with mulled wine, to traditional Mexican street food, Caribbean rubs and Indian curries. I reckon if you cook a few recipes from each chapter you'll end up with a pretty comprehensive understanding of each spice and be confident enough to really start messing around with them on your own. Cooking with spices isn't about making complex spice blends or carefully weighing out and measuring precise quantities, it's about bashing stuff up and throwing it in to transform everyday ingredients into really exciting stuff.

I've also been the guinea pig for several of Emma's spice therapies, aphrodisiacs, perfumes and face packs and I have to admit, they're worth trying. You can sense the power in spices when you chew a clove and your whole mouth goes numb or remember that some of our most powerful drugs come from spices – think of the poppy seeds used to make morphine or the safrole in cinnamon used to make MDMA. It's all good fun and I'm sure some of Emma's tricks will end up as standard therapies in my home and also many of the homes of people who give them a try.

So please don't think that this is a book just to read in bed or put on your coffee table. We wrote it for people to cook from, and that's what we want you to do. No ingredient is too tricky to find and none of the recipes take very long – and they all taste great! So there's really no excuse not to put a bit of spice into your life.

'COOKING WITH SPICES ISN'T ABOUT MAKING COMPLEX SPICE BLENDS OR CAREFULLY WEIGHING OUT AND MEASURING PRECISE QUANTITIES, IT'S ABOUT BASHING STUFF UP AND THROWING IT IN TO TRANSFORM EVERYDAY INGREDIENTS INTO REALLY EXCITING STUFF'

EMMA

Once prized, marvelled at and treasured, spices were revered not just for their exotic colours, heady aromas and the fabulous flavours they imparted to food, but also for their healing properties, and it's high time they reclaimed their rightful spotlight. Cumin, cloves, chillies, black pepper, cinnamon, nutmeg and mace – we've chosen the heavyweights of the spice world to feature in this book. We all know them, some of us love them, and the rest of us will hopefully love them after sharing in our spice trip.

After cooking in restaurant kitchens for years, I went on to develop spiced recipes, therapies and spice blends at The Spicery in Bath. I have always had a real passion for spices and I have enjoyed learning just how much more there is to them than meets the eye. I'm incredibly interested in their holistic value and in getting to the bottom of how to use them effectively: how to store them; cook with them and heal with them; not to mention a wealth of other unexpected and wacky uses I've discovered during our epic adventure. We've explored bustling markets in Istanbul, braved the bugs and beasties in rural Africa and experienced the wonderment of Hindu ceremonies. And we've come back brimming with inspiration and experiences to share – straight from the heart of the islands where spices grow and the people who know them best.

Learning about spices as we've travelled from country to country has been like putting together a jigsaw of world history – exciting doesn't even come close. My favourite anecdote is about how the island of New Amsterdam was sold by the Dutch in exchange for a key nutmeg-growing island. Having acquired New Amsterdam, the British changed its name to New York and the rest is history! We also discovered that Columbus might not have discovered America if he weren't searching for a faster route to the spice islands. The trade of spices played a huge part in building the world as we know it today and it has been mind-blowing realising just how phenomenally important spices have been throughout history, and sometimes deeply moving finding out how and why.

The 'why' must lie in the seemingly magical power of spices to heal, warm, and ignite our senses. They open the door to a world of natural therapies (and we're all shifting in this direction, away from harsh chemicals), being incredibly beneficial to health. Used by the Egyptians, Romans, Greeks, and mentioned in the Bible and ancient Arabic texts, it appears that throughout history they were the key to good health, longevity, love and life, and I was determined to find out more about all these wondrous properties and unravel the folklore surrounding them. It turns out that much of spice folklore seems to be based entirely around the 'magic' of spices and, before the dawn of science, the properties of spices just weren't fully understood, even with modern technology, we still have so much more to learn about them

Today, the research into spices and their properties is really hotting up, and science is proving that, beyond being tasty and smelling great, spices are a valuable and natural way to cure ills and promote health; this makes me jump for joy as I'm all for holistic and natural wherever possible. Not so Mr Stevie Parle. I'm not a qualified medical professional, but I worked closely with an adviser throughout the trip and the remedies I've included in this book have all been thoroughly tested. For all of you who aren't closet hippies (like me), expect a fellow cynic to have road-tested all the spice therapies and happily Foodwise, to me spices say fun, party and people! Food, and especially spiced food, has always meant time for jollity and socialising in my house, both now and growing up. Spices create a sense of the magnificent, bringing drama as the fantastic scents waft through the house wetting everyone's taste buds, while the flavours invigorate and rejuvenate the body. Spiced food is made to be shared for all these reasons. Who wouldn't want to be transported to somewhere exotic and feel more alive! Not only do spices add a welcome shot of colour and flavour to food and drinks (especially cocktails) and create the perfect buzzy dining atmosphere, they also aid digestion of said dinner. Many spices are thought to have aphrodisiac properties as well as improving mental clarity, so you're set to feel elated from your meal in every way. And using spices couldn't be simpler, as my spice blends, quick fixes, everyday recipes and therapies will show you.

C'mon, you don't need any more encouragement to get stuck into the spices, do you?

'WE'VE EXPLORED BUSTLING MARKETS IN ISTANBUL, BRAVED THE BUGS AND BEASTIES IN RURAL AFRICA AND EXPERIENCED THE WONDERMENT OF HINDU CEREMONIES. AND WE'VE COME BACK BRIMMING WITH INSPIRATION AND EXPERIENCES TO SHARE – STRAIGHT FROM THE HEART OF THE ISLANDS WHERE SPICES GROW AND THE PEOPLE WHO KNOW THEM BEST'

CHILLIES

MEXICO

1

'EATING CHILLIES IS A SENSUAL EXPERIENCE – THE HEART RACES, THE MOUTH FEELS THE BURN AND THE BODY COMES ALIVE; IT'S A ROLLER-COASTER ASSAULT ON THE SENSES'

Mexico is the home of chillies and they are grown everywhere there, but it's amazing to think that chillies are a comparatively recent ingredient for many cultures – the Portuguese introduced chillies to Asia just a few hundred years ago, yet it's hard to imagine a lot of Asian cuisines without chilli.

Chillies make food HOT– everyone knows that. But for most of us that is the extent of our understanding. I used to simply add chilli when I wanted to make food spicy, but blowing your head off isn't what it's about at all. Chillies can be used subtly, too: they deliver loads of different flavours and some aren't even particularly hot. Not that being hot is a bad thing, in fact it's really good fun. Spicy food is exciting to eat; it adds an element of danger. Your body thinks it's being poisoned so it produces endorphins, the way it would if you took drugs or when you do loads of exercise or something that makes you feel great. The rush is almost addictive.

Mexicans feel about chillies the way Italians do about pasta: there are strict rules – that only Mexicans can ever really understand – dictating which chilli to use when; and of course, Mama knows best. I'm a little rebellious with the rules but probably just as obsessed. My advice is to buy or grow every chilli possible and start messing around with them. You can't go too far wrong and you'll have a lot of fun on the way. Chilli really is the party spice.

Chillies are vibrant, loud and exciting, and eating them is a sensual experience – the bold reds demand attention, the heart races, the mouth feels the burn and the body comes alive; it's a roller-coaster assault on the senses. The chilli, if it were a person, would be a Beyoncé or Rihanna – fiery, in your face – it will not go unnoticed.

I've always been smitten with Latin culture – the passion, the creativity, the music and the colour, RED, RED, RED! Needless to say, I wasn't disappointed. I found the Mexican people vibrant, warm and possessed of a wonderful zest for life and love, and all that it brings. We were able to share in the Guelaguetza festival of Oaxaca – a beautiful celebration of giving; it was an explosion of colour and sound, with young and old alike on the streets and full of the party spirit.

I cannot imagine a spice other than the chilli lying at the heart of Mexican culture; and it really, truly does. Chillies are embraced here; the kids eat them with gusto (thoroughly putting my chilli tolerance to shame), and we met some lovely ladies who believe that to get a good flavour you must sing and dance when you tend the chillies, and pick them with love. Everyone, and I mean everyone, knows their chillies – their anchos from their habañeros and everything in between; and each chilli is used for a different dish, from delicate and complex concoctions to fiery, slap-you-in-the-face hot. Eating chillies is like tasting a little piece of Mexico – loud, proud, explosive and interesting.

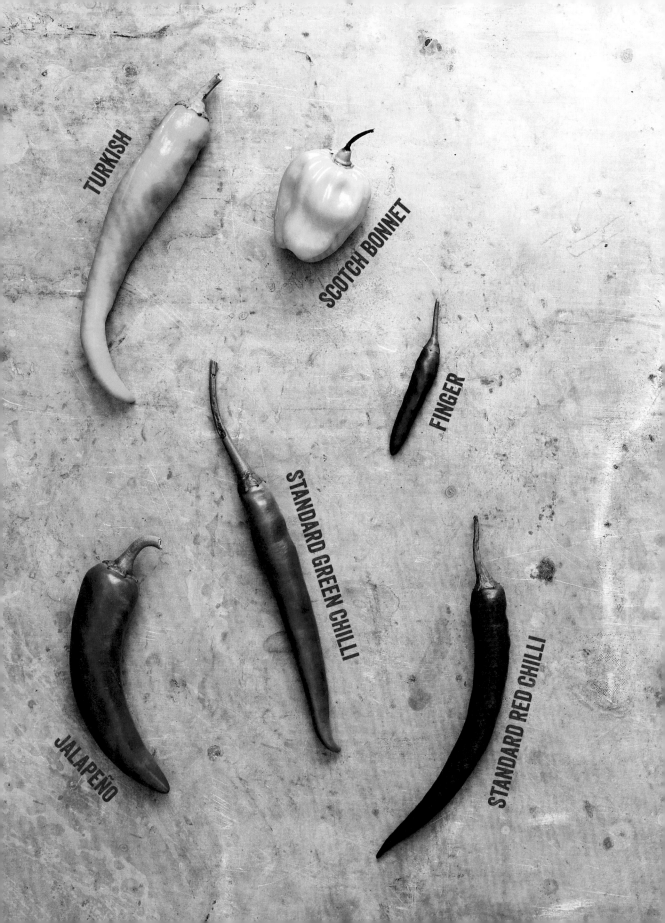

TURKISH

SCOTCH BONNET

FINGER

STANDARD GREEN CHILLI

JALAPEÑO

STANDARD RED CHILLI

GUAJILLO

ANCHO

PASILLA

ARBOL

CHIPOTLE

TURKISH CHILLI FLAKES (PUL BIBER)

QUICK CHILLI-FRIED GREEN BEANS

SERVES FOUR

PREP & COOK: 10 MINS

4 tbsp groundnut oil
400g (14oz) green beans,
   tops trimmed
8 dried Szechuan chillies
   (or other fiery chilli), halved
½ tsp coarsely ground
   Szechuan peppercorns
2.5cm (1in) piece ginger, peeled
   and cut into matchsticks
3 garlic cloves, thinly sliced
2 spring onions, thinly sliced
100g (3½oz) pork mince
sea salt

To serve:
steamed rice

This is one of those recipes that tastes so good, it's hard to believe it contains so few ingredients and is really easy to make. Szechuan pepper isn't actually a pepper, but the dried berries of the prickly ash tree. It's one of the spices in Chinese five-spice and has a lemony aroma and a slightly numbing effect that makes your mouth tingle.

Heat 3 tablespoons of the oil in a wok or large, heavy-based frying pan over a medium heat. Add the beans and stir-fry for 6 minutes until tender and slightly shrivelled. Remove from the pan and set aside.

Wipe the wok clean, add the remaining oil and place back on the heat. Turn the heat up to high, and add the chillies and peppercorns. Stir-fry for 1 minute, then carefully add the ginger, garlic and spring onion. Cook until fragrant, and the ginger and garlic have coloured slightly. Add the pork mince and, when it begins to colour, return the beans to the pan, stir to combine and season with salt to taste. Cook for a few minutes more until the beans are just soft. Serve warm with steamed rice, other Chinese dishes or on its own.

DIVORCED EGGS
SERVES TWO

*For the spicy tomato sauce
(salsa ranchera):*
olive oil
½ red onion, finely chopped
½ garlic clove, finely chopped
1 green or red chilli, seeded
and finely chopped
½ tsp ground allspice
1 x 400g tin plum tomatoes,
drained and rinsed
sea salt and freshly ground
black pepper

For the green apple salsa:
½ Granny Smith apple,
finely chopped
½ cucumber, finely chopped
a handful of coriander leaves,
roughly chopped
2 spring onions, finely chopped
¼ tsp finely chopped green
chilli
juice of 1 lime
sea salt and freshly ground
black pepper

To serve:
4 slices of toast, or 4 corn
tortillas
olive oil, for frying
4 eggs

Huevos divorciados is a common Mexican breakfast dish and is basically jazzy fried eggs. It's so named because the eggs are served with two conflicting sauces: one red and spicy and the other green and cooling. The green apple salsa would usually be made with tomatillos (a relation of physalis), though it works really well here with apple and herbs. Or you could make a more simple salsa by simply dry-roasting guajillo chillies and blending them with water and a garlic clove. For a more substantial meal, serve with refried beans (*frijoles refritos*) and a slice of avocado.

To make the spicy tomato sauce, add some oil to a large pan and gently fry the onion and garlic until soft. Add the chillies and allspice and continue to cook for another minute before adding the tomatoes. Break the tomatoes up with the back of your spoon until you have a smoothish sauce. Season to taste, then leave to simmer with the lid off for 20 minutes until sweet and thickened.

To make the green apple salsa, combine all the ingredients in a small bowl and season to taste.

Add a drizzle of oil to the pan and fry the eggs, either all together or one at a time, depending on the size of your pan. For each serving, place 2 slices of toast, or tortillas, on a plate and top with 2 fried eggs. Spoon the red sauce over one egg and the green sauce over the other.

FLAMING-HOT HABANERO SALSA

PREP: 20 MINS
COOK: 15 MINS

olive oil, for frying
1 red onion, finely chopped
3 garlic cloves, finely chopped
3 Habañero chillies or Scotch
   bonnets, finely chopped
2 carrots, finely chopped
2 bay leaves
½ tsp ground coriander
¼ tsp ground allspice
100ml (3½fl oz) orange juice
30ml (1½fl oz) red wine
   vinegar
1½ tbsp sugar
sea salt and freshly ground
   black pepper

Treat this salsa like Tabasco – add to Bloody Marys or spoon over oysters. Or have manly chilli eating competitions!

Sterilise a 250g (9oz) jar (see page 33).

Heat a splash of oil in a large, heavy-based pan, and gently fry the onion, garlic, chillies, carrots, bay leaves and spices for 15 minutes, until the onions are soft and sweet. Add the orange juice, vinegar and sugar, bring to the boil, then leave to bubble away for 15 minutes, until the liquid has reduced (keep an eye on it to make sure it doesn't catch) and you have a thickish sauce.

Remove the bay leaves, transfer the contents of the pan to a blender (or use a hand blender in the pan) and blend until smooth, adding a little water until you have a loose sauce. Season to taste. Spoon the salsa into your sterilised jar, leaving 1cm (½in) space at the top of the jar, leave to cool and seal tightly. Store in the fridge for up to 2 weeks.

RAW ASPARAGUS
WITH LAMB'S LETTUCE, CHILLI AND MINT

SERVES TWO

PREP: 10 MINS

250g (9oz) asparagus, thinly
   sliced
a handful of mint leaves,
   roughly torn
juice of ½ lemon
extra-virgin olive oil
2 handfuls of lamb's lettuce
1 red chilli, finely sliced
sea salt and freshly ground
   black pepper

You can add some toasted bread, torn into pieces, to this
elegant and simple salad to make a more substantial
plate. Use a speed peeler for lovely thin strips of asparagus.

Place the asparagus strips in a bowl. Season well,
then scatter the mint leaves and squeeze the lemon
juice over the asparagus, along with a splash of oil.

When you're ready to eat, add the lamb's lettuce
and chilli slices, toss gently and serve immediately.

GRILLED SWEETCORN
SOUR CREAM, CHILLI AND CORIANDER

PREP & COOK: 10 MINS

4 cobs sweetcorn, husks
   removed
juice of 1 lime
4 generous tsp sour cream
a handful of coriander leaves,
   roughly torn
dried chilli flakes, to taste
sea salt

Corn is hugely popular in Mexico, where a version of this dish is eaten as street food. My recipe makes a refreshing change from simply boiling your corn and then smothering it in butter.

Heat a griddle pan or barbecue until searingly hot. Place the sweetcorn on the hot griddle or barbecue, and grill until golden and charred all over.

Season the cobs with salt and squeeze the lime juice over them. Dollop a teaspoon of sour cream over each one, scatter with the torn coriander leaves and sprinkle with the dried chilli flakes.

RED PEPPER CHILLI AND WALNUT DIP

SERVES FOUR–SIX

PREP & COOK: 15 MINS

4 red peppers, or 350g (12oz)
   jarred Spanish peppers
70g (2¾oz) walnuts, shelled
½ garlic clove
1 tbsp tahini
1 tbsp ground cumin
1 red chilli, finely chopped
juice of 1–2 lemons, to taste
70g (2¾oz) dried breadcrumbs
3 tbsp olive oil
sea salt and freshly ground
   black pepper

To serve:
warm flatbread or pitta

This wonderful dish, called *cevizli biber* in Turkey, often forms part of a mezze spread, but is also delicious eaten on its own with warm flatbread or pitta. If you can find mild Turkish chilli flakes (*pul biber*), use a teaspoonful of these instead of fresh chilli.

If using fresh peppers, place them on a very hot griddle pan or under a hot grill until the skin is charred and the flesh softened. Transfer to a large bowl, cover with clingfilm and leave to sweat for 10 minutes. Remove from the bowl (retaining any juices), and carefully (they'll be very hot) remove the skin and seeds.

Transfer to a food processor (this can also be done in a pestle and mortar), add the remainder of the ingredients, except the oil, and blitz until smooth, stirring in the oil at the end. Season to taste. Eat with warm flatbread or pitta bread.

GUACAMOLE

PREP: 10 MINS

¼ red onion or 2 spring
  onions, finely chopped
½ garlic clove, roughly
  chopped
2 red or green chillies,
  roughly chopped
3 medium ripe avocados,
  peeled and stoned
juice of 1 lime
a handful of coriander leaves
sea salt

This is how they make guacamole in the markets of Oaxaca. It's simple and delicious. They use huge flat grinding stones to bash the ingredients, but a pestle and mortar or blender work just as well.

Place the onions, garlic and chillies in a pestle and mortar or blender and bash together a bit until they release their juices and are well combined and smooth.

Add the avocado and continue to bash until smooth, then stir in the lime juice, tear in the coriander leaves and season with salt to taste. The guacamole will brown if left to sit, so if you're not serving it immediately, cover the dish with clingfilm until you're ready to eat it.

CHILLI QUICK FIXES

■ A little chilli in vegetable soups or stews (not so much that it's actually hot) keeps you warm in winter.

■ A bit of chilli peps up condiments like tomato ketchup, mayo, oil, barbecue sauce, etc.

■ Make a fresh chilli salsa by blending fresh tomato, diced raw onion, fresh coriander, fresh lime juice and fresh chilli.

■ For a dried chilli salsa, use dried chilli soaked and then blended with dry-fried onion (no oil), garlic and tomato.

■ Slice dried chillies and add to stir-fries and soups for a more complex flavour.

■ Make your own chilli paste by grinding soaked dried chillies to a fine paste.

■ Adding chilli, allspice or cinnamon to any chocolate dish enhances the flavour. They're also great with any dark tobaccoey flavours such as in chilli con carne or beef stew.

Extra tip: You can dry your own chillies by hanging them in your kitchen or a greenhouse, or putting them in a very low oven for several hours. Store in a paper bag to use later, or make chilli oil by adding them to olive oil in a jar or bottle.

CHILLI SPICE BLEND

Chilli works really well with sweet dishes as the sugar counters the fiery heat. It's a great way to introduce kids to spicy food. This blend has a naturally sweet taste and it's great sprinkled over desserts. We added it to popcorn for the kids in Mexico and they also put it on ice cream. You can make an even simpler version by adding a pinch of chilli powder to your hot chocolate at home for an extra-warming, comforting drink.

2-parts ground cinnamon
1-part chilli powder
½-part ground allspice

Uses: Delicious added to hot chocolate; sprinkle generously on popcorn, ice cream, pancakes or waffles with syrup; add to chocolate cake and muffin mixes.

EMMA'S CHILLI LEMON AND GARLIC ROAST POTATOES

SERVES 6–8

PREP: 10 MINS
COOK: APPROX. 40 MINS

1kg (2¼lb) waxy potatoes,
    cut into equal-sized chunks
4 garlic cloves, slightly
    crushed with skins on
whole peel and juice of
    1 lemon
a few sprigs of fresh thyme
    or rosemary
1 tbsp dried chilli flakes,
    or to taste
olive oil
sea salt

This is my roast potato quick fix; new potatoes with skin would be my choice. There's a touch of heat balanced with the earthy sweetness of roast garlic, all lifted with a hint of tangy lemon. It's a fast and punchy way of livening up a Sunday roast, or you could leave the potatoes to cool and then add to a salad of leafy greens, tuna, peas and green beans. Use thick peel from half a lemon or cut the lemon into slices, to prevent it burning in the roasting tin.

Preheat the oven to 190°C/375°F/gas 5.

In a roasting tin, toss the potatoes together with the garlic, lemon peel, thyme or rosemary, dried chilli flakes, a glug of olive oil and a good pinch of salt, then spread the potatoes out so that they cook evenly in the pan.

Roast them for 40 minutes, or until brown. Drizzle with lemon juice before serving.

SALTY CHILLI MARGARITA WITH SPICY CASHEWS AND CHILLI POPPERS

PREP & COOK: 20 MINS

For the spicy cashews:

300g (11oz) cashew nuts
1 lemongrass stem, tough
   outer layer discarded
1 red chilli
1 tbsp sugar
sea salt

For the chilli poppers:

2 egg whites
170ml (6fl oz) sparkling water
150g (5oz) plain flour
120g (4½oz) drained pickled
   chillies (see page 33 for
   recipe), green or red or a
   mixture
vegetable oil, for frying
sea salt

My take on a margarita tastes even better accompanied by these brilliant snacks. You don't always have to think of chilli as a spice or condiment – it can be the main attraction, like these chilli poppers. Great for a party or just as a pick-me-up.

First make the spicy cashews. Preheat the oven to 180°C/350°F/gas 4. Line a baking tray with greaseproof paper. Arrange the nuts on the tray and place in the oven for 5 minutes until warmed through. Remove from the oven and turn it down to 150°C/300°F/gas 2.

Meanwhile, in a pestle and mortar, bash together the lemongrass and red chilli until you have a coarse paste. Transfer to a large bowl, then add the sugar and a generous pinch of salt. Mix well, then toss in the warmed cashews and mix to coat.

Tip the nuts back onto the baking tray and return to the oven for 5 minutes until the coating has hardened slightly. Leave to cool and serve with an extra sprinkling of salt, if necessary.

To make the chilli poppers, first whisk the egg whites until you have stiff peaks. In a separate bowl, pour in the water and whisk in the flour until you have a paste. Fold the whisked egg whites into the flour mixture and season with a little salt.

Heat 5cm (2in) of oil in a large, deep, heavy-based pan over a medium heat. Test the heat of the oil with a chunk of bread; when it sizzles and turns golden after 30 seconds, the oil is hot enough. Dip the chillies into the batter, then very carefully lower them, one by one,

For the salty chilli margarita:

100ml (3½fl oz) tequila
50ml (2fl oz) shot Cointreau
    or triple sec
50ml (2fl oz) lime juice
a large pinch of dried chilli
    flakes, bashed with 4 tsp
    sea salt

To serve:
ice cubes or crushed ice
wedges of fresh lime
4 martini glasses

PREP: 10 MINS

250g (9oz) table salt
30 chillies, red, green or
    a mixture (use the standard
    large green and red chillies
    you find in any
    supermarket)

For the pickling liquid:
1 litre (1¾ pints) red wine
    vinegar
5 tsp table salt
1 tsp coriander seeds
3 bay leaves
2 tbsp sugar

into the hot oil (you will need to do this in batches). When they begin to turn golden (about 2 minutes), remove with a slotted spoon and drain on kitchen paper. Serve with a sprinkling of salt.

To make the margarita, combine all the liquids over ice in a cocktail shaker or a clean jam jar and shake vigorously for about a minute.

Prepare your glasses by rubbing a cut piece of lime around the rim and rolling the rims in a saucer filled with the chilli-salt mixture. Carefully pour in the cocktail and serve immediately.

TO MAKE YOUR OWN PICKLED CHILLIES:
This is really easy to do at home. To sterilise the jars, wash them in warm soapy water, then rinse well and place in a hot oven (220°C/425°F/gas 7) for 10 minutes, or fill with boiling water and leave for 10 minutes, then dry.

Boil the salt in 1 litre (1¾ pints) water. Leave to cool, then drop in your chillies and cover with a plate to keep them submerged. Leave to brine overnight. The following morning, drain the chillies and discard the brine. Prick a few holes in each chilli, using the tip of a sharp knife and divide between sterilised jars.

Bring the pickling liquid ingredients and 1 litre (1¾ pints) of water to boil in a large pan over a high heat then pour over the chillies, filling each jar to the brim. Leave to cool, then serve or seal and store for up to 4 weeks.

CHILLI RULES

There are hundreds of different varieties of chilli: from the frighteningly hot naga that is barely classifiable as food, to the wonderful delicate dried ancho whose mild apricot-like flavour would please even the staunchest of chilliphobes – it's so fruity you can almost put it on your muesli. And there are loads of wonderful different Mexican chillies that are easy to get online. They're great for adding smoky depth and sweetness to almost any cuisine, not just Mexican food: a chipotle chucked into a tomato sauce totally transforms it. Try adding a pinch of dried chilli flakes to all sorts of recipes that you wouldn't expect to find them in, from Italian soups to English stews – and you'll find they don't taste hot at all, just a bit fuller, a bit more interesting and a lot more delicious. Chillies have a magical power that quite simply makes food taste better.

FRESH, DRIED OR POWDERED?

Fresh chillies – have a zingy fresh citrus flavour

Cayenne pepper – finely ground hot chilli varieties, includes the seeds and core making it very fiery.

Chilli powder – milder than cayenne, more coarsely ground, doesn't include seeds. The chilli powders in your spice rack will be labelled mild or hot depending on the heat and flavour of the chillies used. For best results, make your own by dry frying whole dried chillies in a heavy pan, and grinding in a pestle and mortar.

Paprika – made from the mildest chillies, the core and seeds are removed first, then the flesh is dried and powdered. Its flavour is released by heat, but because it contains a lot of sugar it can burn easily. Best to fry your onions and garlic, turn down the heat and then add the paprika.

STORAGE

Fresh chilli has a long shelf life; you can store peppers in the fridge for several weeks.

Dried chillies can be kept in an air-tight container (or at least 'moisture-tight') and away from strong light for up to a year. They will lose their sparkle eventually, but will retain their flavour and colour much better than ground chilli powder.

Chilli powders slowly lose their flavour and colour after a few months. Store in the dark.

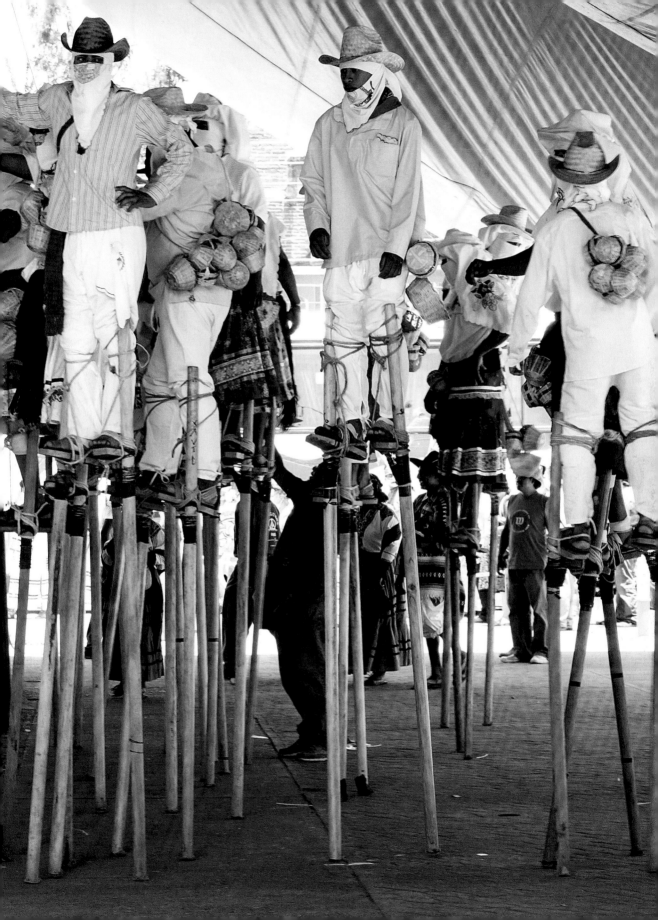

THAI FRIED CHICKEN
WITH SWEET CHILLI SAUCE

SERVES FOUR–SIX

PREP & COOK: 30 MINS

2 tsp Szechuan peppercorns
5 star anise
5 cloves
2.5cm (1in) cinnamon stick
1 tbsp anise seeds
¼ tsp black peppercorns
1 tsp fennel seeds
150g (5oz) plain flour,
    seasoned with sea salt
2 eggs, beaten
1 x 1.5kg (3¼lb) chicken,
    jointed with backbone
    and wing tips removed
vegetable oil, for frying
sea salt, to sprinkle

For the sweet chilli sauce:
2 red bird's-eye chillies,
    very finely chopped
½ garlic clove, crushed
100ml (3½fl oz) rice wine
    vinegar
6 tbsp sugar
2 tbsp fish sauce

This is my twist on everyone's favourite fried chicken.
The spice mix makes it really aromatic and is perfectly
offset by the sweet chilli sauce.

Make the chilli sauce first. Place all the sauce ingredients
except the fish sauce in a pan, bring to the boil and leave
to simmer for 5 minutes until slightly thickened. Stir in
the fish sauce and leave to cool.

To make the chicken, toast the Szechuan peppercorns
for 1 minute in a dry pan, then combine with the other
spices in a pestle and mortar or a spice grinder and
grind into a fine powder. Put to one side.

Combine the flour and a quarter of the spice mix in
a bowl. Place the eggs in a separate bowl. Scatter the
remaining spice mix over a large plate. Roll the chicken
joints, one at a time, in the spice mix, then dip them
in the beaten egg and then in the flour. Shake off any
excess flour.

In a large, deep cast-iron frying pan, add enough oil to
come about one-third up the sides of the pan. Heat the oil
to about 180°C (test by adding a cube of bread; if it sizzles
and turns golden in 30 seconds, the oil is hot enough).

Carefully fry the chicken in batches, being careful not
to crowd the pan. Turn the meat over once the underside
is golden. When the chicken is cooked through and
perfectly juicy with an all-over golden, crunchy crust, it's
done. Be aware that the breast will cook quicker, so you
might need to leave the dark meat in for a moment longer.
Drain on kitchen paper, sprinkle over a little sea salt,
and serve with the chilli sauce.

CHILLI FISH STEW

SERVES TWO

PREP: 15 MINS
COOK: 20 MINS

olive oil
1 red onion, finely chopped
1 celery stick, finely chopped
1 fennel bulb, tough outer
   layer removed (reserve
   the fronds) and flesh finely
   chopped
1 garlic clove, finely chopped
2 mild red chillies, finely
   chopped
a pinch of dried chilli flakes
2 tomatoes, roughly chopped
400ml (14fl oz) white wine
2 x 125g (4¾oz) monkfish
   fillets or other firm
   white fish
2 x 125g (4¾oz) red mullet
   or red snapper fillets
200g (7½oz) clams, scrubbed
   and rinsed
200g (7½oz) mussels, scrubbed
   and rinsed with beards
   removed
4 large whole raw prawns,
   shell on
a handful of parsley leaves,
   roughly chopped
sea salt and freshly ground
   black pepper

To serve:
2 thick slices bread, toasted

This is a really easy and brilliant fish stew that's perfect for any occasion from a quick supper to a party or even for Christmas if you aren't into a traditional roast. Add lobster or prawns to make it feel more celebratory, or use cheaper fish and mussels for a more frugal version. The chilli lifts the whole dish and makes it a really exciting thing to eat. I love having the background warmth of dried chilli and the kick of fresh chilli oil.

Heat some oil in a large, wide heavy-based pan (with a lid). Gently fry the onion, celery, fennel, garlic and half the chopped chilli with a pinch each of salt and dried chilli flakes until soft, about 8 minutes. Stir in the tomatoes and a dash of water and continue to cook for 5 minutes.

Turn the heat up and pour in the wine. Turn down and leave to simmer for 3 minutes until the liquid has slightly reduced.

Cut the fish into large chunks, season well, and add in a single layer, pushing the pieces down so they are covered by the liquid. Cook gently for 3 minutes, then add the clams, mussels and prawns. Stir gently to combine, then place the lid on the pan and leave to steam for 3 minutes until the clams and mussels have opened and the prawns are cooked through. (Discard any clams or mussels that don't open.)

Place the remaining chilli in a small bowl and cover generously with oil. Divide the fish stew between 2 bowls, sprinkle with the parsley and fennel fronds and spoon the chilli oil on top. Serve with toast drizzled with oil.

CHILLIES
LARGE
PLATES

SMOKY PULLED PORK AND SLAW

**PREP: 30 MINS
COOK: 5 HRS**

½ shoulder of pork, (about
   2kg/4½lb) off the bone
250ml (8fl oz) dry cider or
   apple juice
olive oil
sea salt and freshly ground
   black pepper

For the dry rub:
2 tbsp fennel seeds
1 tbsp black peppercorns
1 dried chilli or 2 tsp dried
   chilli flakes
2 chipotle or ancho chillies,
   chopped
2 garlic cloves
½ tbsp coriander seeds
½ tbsp cumin seeds
1 tbsp smoked paprika
2 tbsp brown sugar

For the barbecue sauce:
400ml (14fl oz) tomato passata
1 tbsp Dijon mustard
2 tbsp sugar
60ml (2½fl oz) cider vinegar

For the coleslaw:
½ white cabbage, finely sliced
1 bunch (about 300g/11oz)
   radishes, finely sliced
4 spring onions, finely sliced
2 green apples, finely sliced
2 handfuls each of coriander
   and mint leaves
juice of 2 limes
olive oil
sea salt and freshly ground
   black pepper

This dish is seriously rewarding. You may want to cook it overnight, or start it in the morning so it's ready in time for dinner. It doesn't take too long to set up and the final result is worth the wait. If you can't find chipotle or ancho chillies, add an extra tablespoonful of paprika instead.

Preheat the oven to 220°C/425°F/gas 7. Grind the dry rub ingredients in a pestle and mortar until coarse. Remove the skin from the pork and discard or use for crackling.

Sprinkle the pork generously with salt. In a deep, flameproof casserole (with lid), heat a good glug of oil and when hot, brown the pork on both sides. Remove from the casserole and cover with the dry rub, making sure you get it in all the nooks and crannies. Drain the excess fat from the casserole and return the pork to it. Pour the cider or apple juice over the pork. Bake in the oven, uncovered, for 20 minutes, then reduce the oven to 140°C/275F/gas 1, cover and cook for a further 3½–5 hours, until the meat is soft and pulls apart easily. Top up with extra cider, juice or water if necessary.

Remove from the oven. Take the pork out and place on a plate or board. Place the casserole over a high heat and bring to the boil. Add the barbecue sauce ingredients and season to taste. Turn the heat down and leave to bubble for 10–15 minutes, until it has thickened and reduced a little. Meanwhile, pull the pork apart with two forks so it's nicely shredded.

Make the coleslaw by combining the cabbage, radishes, spring onions and apples. Tear the herbs over it and squeeze in the lime juice, along with a small drizzle of oil. Season to taste.

Pour the barbecue sauce over the pork and serve with the coleslaw.

ROASTED SWEET CHILLI LAMB

SERVES FOUR

PREP: 30 MINS
COOK: 10–15 MINS

4 chipotle chillies
boiling water, to cover
3 garlic cloves
1 red or white onion
400ml (14fl oz) tomato passata
2 tbsp dark brown sugar
1 tbsp sherry vinegar
4 x 200g (7oz) lamb rump
    steaks
sea salt and freshly ground
    black pepper

YOU WILL NEED:

jalapeño chillies
presoaked hardwood chips
(e.g. apple, cherry or beech)

If you can't find chipotle chillies, you can substitute them with a teaspoonful of smoked paprika — or even smoke them at home (see below). If you keep the dried chipotle intact while cooking it will imbue the sauce with flavour but not heat. Puncture it and you'll get heat; chop it and you'll get fire!

In a dry frying pan, toast the chipotles lightly on both sides. When cool enough to handle, remove the stems and seeds and tear the flesh into pieces. Place in a bowl and pour in enough boiling water to cover the chillies. Leave to soak for 30 minutes.

Preheat the oven to 180°C/350°F/gas 4. Place the chillies, and their soaking water, in a food processor or pestle and mortar, add the garlic, onion, tomatoes, brown sugar and vinegar and blend to a coarse purée. Season to taste and rub into the lamb steaks.

Place the lamb on a baking tray and season with a little salt. Roast for 10–15 minutes, brushing the meat with the sauce every few minutes. When cooked, leave to rest for a few minutes before serving with with greens and roast potatoes.

SMOKING YOUR OWN CHIPOTLE CHILLIES

This is easy to do with a hooded barbecue. Split the chillies, remove and discard the seeds and spread the chillies out over the grill. Pull down the hood, leaving a gap for the smoke to circulate, and leave to smoke slowly for 5–6 hours.

FRESH GREEN FISH CURRY

PREP: 20 MINS
COOK: 15–20 MINS

juice of 6 limes
a pinch of turmeric
900g (2lb) hake or other firm
  white fish, cut into chunks
2 tbsp poppy seeds
100g (3½oz) freshly grated
  coconut
8–10 whole green chillies,
  stems removed
1 red onion
5 garlic cloves
50g (2oz) cashew nuts
6 green cardamoms, seeds
  removed and shells
  discarded
1 tsp ground cinnamon
½ tsp fennel seeds
olive oil
2 tsp cumin seeds
2 tsp coriander seeds, ground
  and mixed with a little
  water to make a paste
150g (5oz) coriander leaves
  and stalks
a large handful of mint leaves
sea salt and freshly ground
  black pepper

To serve:
steamed rice

This recipe is based on one from Camellia Panjabi's classic cookbook *50 Great Curries of India* and is wonderfully light, but packs a serious, spicy punch. The sauce also goes well with chicken.

Combine half the lime juice with the turmeric, a good pinch of salt and a dash of water and rub over the fish. Leave to marinate for 20 minutes.

Meanwhile, grind the poppy seeds in a pestle and mortar with a dash of water. Transfer to a food processor with the coconut, chillies, onion, garlic, cashew nuts, cardamom, cinnamon and fennel seeds and grind everything together until you have a thick paste. Remove and put to one side.

Heat a good glug of oil in a large, wide, heavy-based pan. Add the cumin seeds and when they begin to gently sizzle, add the ground coriander seed paste. After about 10 seconds, add the spice paste and fry gently for 7 minutes, stirring constantly to prevent sticking.

Meanwhile, place the coriander and mint leaves in the food processor and purée. Add to the spice mixture, followed by the remaining lime juice. Season to taste, pour in 300ml (½ pint) water and bring to the boil. Add the fish and reduce the heat to a simmer. Cook for 7–10 minutes, until the fish is cooked through. Serve with rice.

MY GREEN CHILLI CON CARNE

SERVES SIX–EIGHT

PREP: 15 MINS
COOK: 10–15 MINS

olive oil
800g (1¾lb) pork or beef
  mince, or a mixture
2 handfuls sage leaves,
  chopped
2 onions, roughly chopped
3 garlic cloves, finely sliced
2 green peppers, seeded and
  roughly chopped
6 green chillies, roughly
  chopped
4 large tomatoes, roughly
  chopped
½ bunch each of mint,
  coriander and oregano,
  leaves picked (save a few
  coriander leaves for the
  garnish)
juice of 1 lime
4 spring onions, finely sliced
sea salt and freshly ground
  black pepper

To serve:
4 flour tortillas, warmed
sour cream

You really want to use tomatillos (a relation of physalis) for this *chile verde*, but in their absence, the combination of tomatoes and green peppers is fine. This is great served with the Green Apple Salsa (see page 19).

Heat a good glug of olive oil in a large pan over a medium heat. Add the mince, sage and a good pinch of salt and pepper. Cook for a few minutes until coloured, stirring occasionally. Transfer to a bowl.

In the same pan, add some more oil, then add the onions, garlic, peppers and chillies and fry for 15 minutes over a medium heat until soft. Return the meat to the pan, and continue cooking for another 5 minutes. Stir in the tomatoes – it should be pretty dry, but add a little water if you're worried. Turn the heat down and leave to bubble for about 10–15 minutes.

Meanwhile, in a blender, whiz together the mint, coriander and oregano with a pinch of salt until you have a green paste. Squeeze in the lime, then stir this into the meat, followed by the spring onions. Garnish with the reserved coriander leaves. Serve with warm tortillas, a dollop of sour cream and the Green Apple Salsa if you fancy.

EMMA'S TROPICAL LIME AND CHILLI POSSET
WITH CRUSHED PISTACHIOS AND RASPBERRIES

SERVES FOUR

PREP: 10 MINS
SETTING: 3 HRS+

350ml (12fl oz) double cream
juice of 4 limes and zest of 3
220g (7½oz) sugar
4–6 red chillies, seeded
    and thinly sliced
a couple of handfuls of
    raspberries
a small handful of crushed
    pistachios

A posset has to be one of the quickest pudding fixes, as long as you leave time for it to set. Lime gives a milder, sweeter flavour than the traditional lemon, which makes for a gentler flavour combination with the chilli. The chillies need to be quite hot for this dish because the sugar and dairy will counteract the heat. The raspberries cut through the indulgent creaminess, and together with the crushed pistachios, give wonderful texture and colour. This one's a real looker for dinner parties.

Combine the cream, lime zest and 120g (4½oz) of the sugar in a pan. Bring to the boil, then immediately turn the heat right down and let it simmer on the lowest setting for 5 minutes or until the sugar has totally dissolved, stirring to prevent the cream burning at the bottom. Stir in the lime juice, bring back to the boil and just as it starts to bubble up, take it off the heat. Strain the hot liquid through a sieve into 4 wide glasses or cups. Chill for several hours (preferably overnight) to allow it to set.

To make the chilli syrup, combine the remaining 100g (4oz) sugar in a pan with 100ml (3½fl oz) water and an extra squeeze of lime. Heat slowly until the sugar has dissolved. Add the sliced chillies and simmer until the liquid becomes syrupy, then leave to cool. Add a little water if it gets so sticky you can't get it out of the pan!

Serve the posset straight from the fridge, with a good tablespoon of chilli syrup over the top, sprinkled with raspberries and topped with crushed pistachios – like a fancy sundae.

REALLY EASY CHOCOLATE CAKE
WITH CHILLI, SALT AND TEQUILA

SERVES TWELVE

PREP: 15 MINS
COOK: 20 MINS

200g (7oz) dark chocolate with
   70 per cent cocoa solids
200g (7oz) butter
2 tsp dried chilli flakes
4 eggs
150g (5oz) sugar
4 tbsp ground almonds
1 tbsp plain flour
a pinch of sea salt
2 tbsp tequila, plus a little
   extra to serve

This cake is unbelievably easy to make. It came about through a bungled attempt by one of my chefs to make a cake. Mumbled, distracted instructions produced an unorthodox technique which gave rise to a brilliantly simple cake recipe (mix it all together in one bowl and bake it!). I'm really glad I said 'Bake it, let's see what happens' to that particular error.

Preheat the oven to 180°C/350°F/gas 4. Grease a 23cm (9in) round cake tin and line with baking paper.

Melt the chocolate, butter and chilli in a glass or metal bowl over a pan of barely simmering water (or in a microwave). The bowl must not touch the water as this will split the mixture. Remove from the heat, stir and leave for a few minutes to cool slightly.

Stir in the eggs one by one, then the sugar, followed by the almonds, flour, a pinch of salt and the tequila. Pour the batter into the cake tin and sprinkle over a generous amount of salt. Bake for 20—25 minutes, or until an inserted skewer comes out clean.

Leave to cool and just before you serve, drizzle a little tequila over each slice.

EMMA'S TOMATO CHILLI JAM

MAKES 250G (9OZ)

WITH GINGER AND FRESH CORIANDER

PREP: 15 MINS
COOK: 1 HR

500g (1¼lb) really ripe
   tomatoes, roughly chopped
4 garlic cloves, finely chopped
1 heaped tbsp finely chopped
   ginger
6 red chillies, seeded,
   and finely sliced
juice of 2 limes
300g (11oz) sugar
100ml (3½fl oz) red wine
   or rice wine vinegar
3 star anise
½ tsp table salt
a small handful of chopped
   coriander

This is a hodgepodge of recipes that I've acquired from friends and refined into a kind of half salsa, half jam that you can happily drizzle over seafood, rice, chicken and salads. It's not seriously hot as the heat is calmed by the sugar – you can up the heat by leaving the seeds in the chillies. It's tangy, fresh and lively. I eat it with everything!

Sterilise your jars (see page 33). Coarsely blitz the tomatoes, garlic and ginger in a blender.

Put the blitzed tomato mixture into a pan and add the remainder of the ingredients, except the coriander. Bring to the boil and then turn down the heat to a simmer. Leave to simmer for 40–50 minutes, stirring to avoid the mixture sticking, until it becomes a thicker, more jam-like consistency.

To test if it's ready, pop a saucer into the fridge for a couple of minutes. Spoon a little chilli jam onto it, leave to cool, then smear your finger through it – the surface will wrinkle if the jam is at setting point. If the jam isn't ready, continue to simmer and then repeat the saucer test.

At the last moment, stir in the fresh coriander and ladle the jam into the sterilised jars, leaving 1cm (½in) space at the top of the jar. Leave to cool, seal the jars tightly and store in the fridge.

EMMA'S CHILLI THERAPIES

In astrology, chilli peppers are considered part of the dominion of Mars, god of war, and it's easy to see where this aggressive reputation comes from. The Incas believed chilli peppers to be a disruptive influence so chillies were banned from initiation and funeral ceremonies. Chillies are a full-on assault on the senses but they encourage 'excitement' as opposed to disruption, which is a good thing in my book – if you want a lively dinner party, be sure to add chillies. In the Amazon, chilli is sometimes added to 'yage' mixtures – hallucinogenic medicines that shamans use for healing rituals.

Fresh chilli peppers are extremely high in vitamin C, containing 94mg per 74g, compared with 37mg in oranges. Drying chillies reduces their vitamin C content, but increases the level of vitamin A by 100 times. So fresh or dried – it's a win–win situation. Antioxidants help protect the body against the damaging and ageing effects of free radicals. Chillies also contain flavonoids, which makes them a powerful source of antioxidants .

THE STORY OF CHILLIES

Christopher Columbus found chillies on his first voyage to the Americas in 1492 and called them 'peppers' because they were hot and spicy like black pepper, although chillies are technically fruits and completely unrelated to pepper. Which of the myriad varieties he found and took back to Spain six years later remains a mystery, though it's commonly believed it was the piri-piri chilli pepper, which then grew in such abundance in West Africa that it was often mistaken for a native plant. All chillies, however, originated in South America. Chillies spread around the world fast – in the space of just 50 years. Between 1498 and 1549, they travelled the globe: eastwards out of Spain and Portugal to China, India and Japan; and westwards from Mexico through the Philippines to the Far East. All the more amazing considering the methods of transportation at the time.

A NOTE OF WARNING

In extreme cases, consumed chillies may cause a rash. Use them carefully. Because the capsaicin in chillies is doesn't dissolve in H^2O, water is no use to quell the fire! But foods rich in fat, such as yoghurt or milk, or a sweet food like honey – or even alcohol – will take the edge off the heat.

It goes without saying that getting chilli in your eye is something to be avoided. After handling chillies, always wash your hands thoroughly in warm soapy water.

MEDICINAL USES

■ Chillies are rich in B vitamins such as niacin, pyridoxine (vitamin B-6), riboflavin and thiamin (vitamin B-1), which are important for maintaining energy levels.

■ Chillies contain Vitamins C and E, and pro Vitamin A. However, they tend to lose their vitamin content when cooked or pickled or if they ripen too much.

■ The chilli has been used for centuries in folk medicine as an aphrodisiac. Its fiery nature ignites the flame of passion – or so it is said.

■ The active constituents found in chillies are, surprisingly, used as an antispasmodic and to soothe, as in some cough preparations or over-the-counter muscle rubs. They are also used to ease chest congestion.

■ In some traditions the whole plant is cooked in milk and applied to the body to reduce swellings.

■ Chilli is said to be an effective fumigant for bed bugs and rats, should the need arise.

■ Chilli helps improve digestion by increasing the body's production of saliva. It is a carminative.

■ Chilli can be used externally as a local irritant to counter other irritants, itching or pain, although if you've ever had a hot chilli all over your hands you would agree this is not an advisable use for it.

■ Tear gas and pepper spray contain chilli, and it is used as a crop deterrent against elephants in Africa and South Asia. This is a great tip if you're ever faced with a rampaging stampede.

CHILLI HANGOVER CURE/WINTER CURE-ALL

This is halfway between a soup and a savoury tea – it's pretty potent so you don't need a whole mugful. The stock is wholesome, the ginger soothes nausea and the cinnamon and chilli improve circulation, helping the body to work faster at relieving the crisis. Meanwhile, the coriander and chilli are anti-inflammatory, effectively calming headaches, and the sugar and salt help restore the body's natural balance. Not only will this give you a serious kick-start, it can also help ward off colds and flu that the body is more susceptible to when rundown after a long night.

Serves 4 mildly hungover people or 2 who've
   REALLY overdone it
2 pieces of chicken on the bone
a thumb's length of ginger, sliced
2 garlic cloves, sliced
1 white onion, sliced
1 carrot, chopped
1 cinnamon stick, broken up
1 tbsp coriander seeds, roasted
2 tsp dried chilli flakes or 1 fresh red chilli, sliced
1–2 tsp sugar or honey, or to taste
½ tsp sea salt, or to taste
a squeeze of fresh lemon juice or a little red
   wine vinegar

Place the chicken in a large pan. Add 1 litre (1¾ pints) water, ginger, garlic, onion, carrot, cinnamon, coriander seeds and chilli and simmer for about 20 minutes, until the chicken is cooked through.

Carefully remove the chicken with a slotted spoon and allow to cool (continue simmering the stock). When the chicken is cool enough to handle, remove the meat from the bone.

Strain the stock through a sieve into a jug, then return the chicken meat to the pan with the strained stock. Add the sugar or honey, the salt and the lemon juice or vinegar. Sip as much as you can handle!

CHILLI OIL MUSCLE RUB

The compound capsaicin in chillies improves circulation and has a mild pain-relieving action; it also encourages the brain to release endorphins which give the same natural feeling of wellbeing as exercise. Combined with a liniment or oil and applied directly to the skin it can alleviate chest infections like bronchitis.

Used topically, chilli can help to ease pain in rheumatic joints. If you've ever used a muscle rub like Deep Heat you will know how a good, warming rub can help relax and soothe sore muscles, aching joints and arthritic pain.

If you prepare this rub in advance, it'll keep forever. You needn't remove the chillies until you are ready to use it. Do not apply it to broken skin, and avoid any contact with the eye area. Be sure to do a patch test before applying large amounts.

Makes: 1 x 100ml (3½fl oz) bottle or jar

100ml (3½fl oz) oil, such as grapeseed, almond or olive
3 small dried red chillies or fresh red chillies
1 sealable jar or bottle, sterilised (see page 33)

Simply combine the oil and chillies in your sterilised jar or bottle. Seal tightly and allow to infuse for several days, preferably in a sunny spot. The oil will eventually take on the red of the chillies.

Apply directly to the affected area, avoiding broken skin, massaging it well. Alternatively, you can make a poultice by soaking a bandage in the chilli oil and wrapping an area such as a painful ankle.

NUTMEG & MACE GRENADA

2

'GRENADA IS A WONDERFULLY VIBRANT PLACE; THEY KNOW HOW TO PARTY AND HOW TO EAT, AND NUTMEG REALLY HELPS THEM DO BOTH. IT'S SPRINKLED ON THE RUM PUNCH AND MIXED INTO THE "MANNISH WATERS" AND EVERYONE IS CONVINCED OF ITS MANHOOD-ENHANCING POWERS'

STEVIE

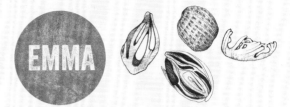

EMMA

I think of nutmeg as the most British of spices – it's the spice of bread sauce, cauliflower cheese, creamed spinach and apple pie – and yet it comes from some of the most beautiful, exotic tropical places on earth.

We went to Grenada to find out more. Grenada is a wonderfully vibrant place; they know how to party and how to eat, and nutmeg really helps them do both. It's sprinkled on the rum punch and mixed into the 'Mannish waters' (a sort of Irish stew made from goat's head) and everyone is convinced of its manhood-enhancing powers. Grenadians are seriously into nutmeg. It's even on their flag.

Nutmeg is one of the most versatile of all the spices. You can put it on almost anything. In fact, I can't think of much that wouldn't benefit from a scratch or two of it. It's often grated on food after cooking, because if you heat nutmeg, it loses some of its wonderful perfumed quality. That said, it retains a lot of its depth and spiciness, so it's still a great spice for seasoning – just remember if you are going for an aromatic, 'pretty' nutmeg taste, you might want to grate a little on at the end.

If you're wondering what the difference between nutmeg and mace is, nutmeg is the seed of the tree *Myristica fragrans*, while mace is its lacy covering. They both have similar qualities, but nutmeg tends to be slightly sweeter and mace has a more delicate flavour. Nutmeg is an immensely comforting spice that has a natural affinity with dairy, so here you will find some of the richer, more wintry recipes in this book.

I was so excited about going to Grenada; I've spent some time in the Caribbean as my dad's from Trinidad, so I knew it would feel the most familiar of all the countries we visited. I also knew we'd be in for a fun time. Caribbean culture embraces the enjoyment of life – of relaxing, enjoying nature ('liming' as it's called), partying, having a jam and always, always eating good, wholesome, home-cooked food.

Grenada did not disappoint. Life seems to bob along to a soca beat. We cooked 'oil down', Grenada's national dish, with some very enthusiastic men on 'oil down corner', Stevie hacked up a goat's head (bleugh!) to make 'Mannish waters' at a cricket game, and we discovered how nutmeg is literally the most versatile spice in the world. It goes in everything. The Grenadians love nutmeg. They all know how to grow it and what healing properties it holds. Indeed, one of their mottoes is 'respec de nutmeg'; everyone we met raved about it and generally fuelled my enthusiasm no end – Stevie had to pacify me with rum punch!

What excites me above all about nutmeg is the phenomenal potential it holds for the future of medicine. It has more than 140 active chemical compounds, some of which our technology is not yet able to fathom. The ones that are understood are remarkable; after suffering an awful achey backpack back for two weeks, I found a nutmeg therapy was the only thing that helped relieve it, and the effect was almost instant.

NUTMEG & MACE INTRODUCTION

EASY TART
OF CHARD, NUTMEG AND OLIVES

•••

**PREP: 25 MINS
+ 1 HR CHILLING
COOK: 20–25 MINS**

olive oil
2 red onions, finely sliced
1 garlic clove, finely sliced
½ bunch thyme, leaves picked
700g (1½lb) Swiss chard
    leaves, boiled, drained
    and chopped
1 egg yolk
3 tbsp crème fraîche
a large handful of freshly
    grated Parmesan
¾ nutmeg, freshly grated
a handful of black olives,
    stoned
6 anchovy fillets
sea salt and freshly ground
    black pepper

For the pastry:
300g (11oz) plain flour,
    plus extra for dusting
a pinch of table salt
150g (5oz) butter, chilled
    and cut into cubes
1 egg yolk

1 x 35 x 29cm (14 x 11½in)
    baking tray

You can also use spinach, fennel, courgette or practically any vegetable here. It's a real 'what's in the fridge?' kind of recipe.

Preheat the oven to 180°C/350°F/gas 4. Grease a 35 x 29cm (14 x 11½in) baking tray.

To make the pastry, sift the flour and a good pinch of salt into a bowl, and combine. Rub in the butter with your fingertips (or mix the flour, salt and butter in a food processor) until the mixture resembles coarse breadcrumbs. Add the egg yolk and combine until the dough just comes together. Shape into a ball, wrap in clingfilm and chill in the fridge for 1 hour.

On a floured surface, roll out the pastry so that it's ½cm (¼in) thick and fits your baking tray. Transfer to the baking tray and chill in the fridge while you prepare the topping.

Heat some oil in a large, heavy-based pan and gently fry the onions, garlic and thyme until caramelised, about 10–15 minutes. Stir in the cooked chard and season well.

In a bowl, beat the egg yolk into the crème fraîche, and stir in the Parmesan and nutmeg. Season with a little pepper.

Spread the chard mixture over the tart base. Scatter the olives over the chard, dollop with generous spoonfuls of the crème fraîche mixture and arrange the anchovies evenly on top. Bake for 20–25 minutes until golden.

ROMAN-STYLE BAKED GNOCCHI WITH FRIED SAGE

SERVES SIX

PREP & COOK: 35 MINS

1 litre (1¾ pints) milk
200g (7oz) semolina
3 egg yolks
150g (5oz) freshly grated
   Parmesan, plus extra
   for serving
120g (4½oz) butter, plus
   extra for greasing
½ nutmeg, freshly grated
prosciutto slices (optional),
   to serve
sea salt and freshly ground
   black pepper

For the fried sage:
40g (1½oz) butter
1 bunch sage, leaves picked

This is proper comfort food. It takes a bit of elbow grease at the beginning, but it is well worth it in the end and means your gnocchi won't fall apart.

In a large pan, bring the milk to the boil. Turn down to a medium-low heat, then whisk in the semolina. Continue to cook, stirring constantly with a wooden spoon for 10 minutes. The mixture should be very thick, so don't be tempted to add more milk.

Take the pan off the heat and stir in the egg yolks, one at a time, making sure each one is incorporated before adding the next. Stir in the Parmesan, the butter and the nutmeg and season well.

Line a shallow roasting tin with greaseproof paper, then pour in the gnocchi mixture. Spread the mixture with the back of a spoon so that you have an even thickness of 2cm (¾in). Leave to cool.

Preheat the oven to 200°C/400°F/gas 6. Line 2 baking trays with greaseproof paper, then butter the paper. Cut the cooled gnocchi into 4cm (1½in) squares and carefully transfer to the baking trays, leaving a 2cm (¾in) space between each one. Grate a little extra Parmesan over the gnocchi and bake in the oven for 15 minutes until golden.

Meanwhile, prepare the fried sage by melting the butter in a frying pan and when it begins to sizzle, add the sage leaves. Cook for a few seconds until crisp. Scatter the sage leaves over the gnocchi before serving. Delicious with thin slices of prosciutto.

SIMPLE OLD-SCHOOL NUTMEG SPINACH SOUFFLÉ

SERVES SIX

PREP: 18 MINS
COOK: 35–50 MINS
DEPENDING ON DISH

125g (4¾oz) butter, plus
   extra for greasing
250g (9oz) freshly grated
   Parmesan, plus extra for
   dusting and sprinkling
½ onion, finely chopped
500g (1¼lb) spinach, boiled,
   drained and finely chopped
500ml (18fl oz) milk
50g (2oz) plain flour, sifted
¾ nutmeg, freshly grated
6 eggs, separated, at room
   temperature
sea salt and freshly ground
   black pepper

1 x 23cm (9in) soufflé or
   casserole dish or 6 x small
   ramekins

People always think of a soufflé as really hard to make, but it isn't. You just have to follow the instructions and not mess around with it when it's in the oven. Sweet nutmeg is a classic partner to earthy spinach, so this recipe works really well.

Preheat the oven to 200°C/400°F/gas 6. Generously butter a 23cm (9in) soufflé or casserole dish or 6 small ramekins. Dust with a little Parmesan and place on a baking tray.

Melt 50g (2oz) of the butter in a large, heavy-based pan. Add the onion and gently fry until soft. Add the chopped spinach and cook for another minute until the spinach is warmed through. Transfer the spinach mixture to a blender or food processor with 100ml (3½fl oz) of the milk and blend until smooth. Push though a sieve so that you have a purée. Season to taste.

Bring the remainder of the milk to the boil, then take off the heat. Make a béchamel sauce by melting the remaining butter in a large, heavy-based pan over a low to medium heat. Whisk in the flour and gently cook, stirring, until it begins to foam, about 3 minutes. Slowly whisk in the milk and stir vigorously until you have a smooth, thick mixture. Stir in the spinach purée and the nutmeg, and season to taste. Leave to cool.

In a clean bowl, beat the egg whites with a pinch of salt until soft peaks form. Beat the yolks into the cooled béchamel mixture, one at a time, then fold in a quarter of the whites. Stir in the 250g (9oz) Parmesan, then fold the soufflé mixture into the remaining egg whites. Don't over-mix.

Spoon the soufflé mixture into your prepared dish or divide between your ramekins, and sprinkle a little Parmesan over the top. Run a knife or thumb around the edge of the dish or ramekins – this will encourage the soufflé to rise. Bake for 20–25 minutes if using a large dish, or 10–15 minutes for individual ramekins. Do not open the oven during cooking, or your soufflé will collapse!

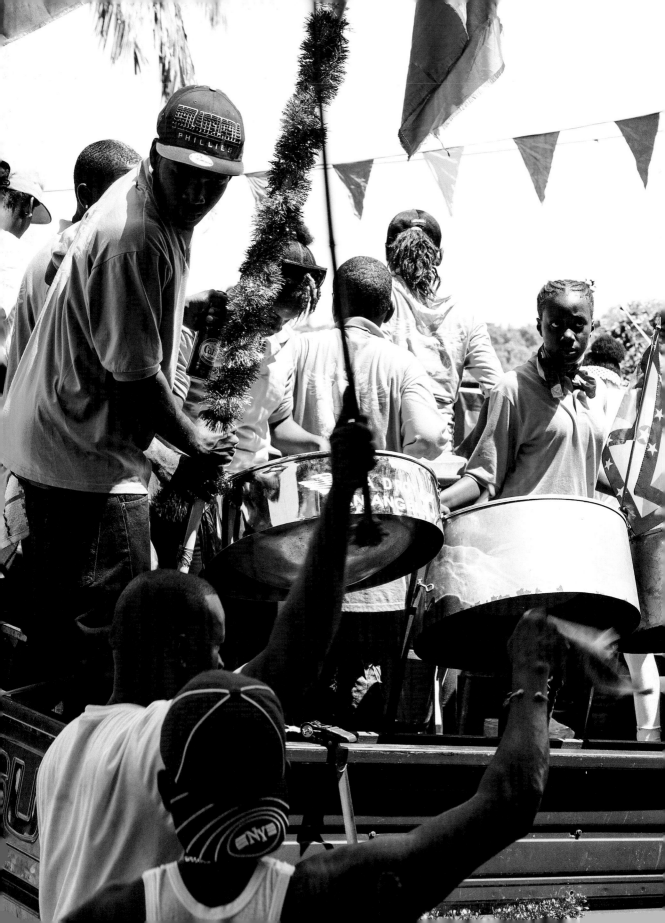

EMMA'S MAC & CHEESE

SERVES FOUR

PREP: 30 MINS
COOK: 30 MINS

500g (16oz) dried macaroni
50g (2oz) butter
2 heaped tbsp plain flour
3 garlic cloves, finely sliced
4 bay leaves
1 litre (1¾ pints) milk
½ nutmeg, freshly grated
1 tbsp mustard powder
½ tsp smoked paprika
¼ tsp dried thyme
175g (6oz) each of strong
   Cheddar and Parmesan,
   grated
2 eggs, lightly beaten
2 tomatoes, thinly sliced
sea salt and freshly ground
   black pepper

To serve:
hot pepper sauce

A staple in any Caribbean and American soul food kitchen, this is real home cooking. The difference between regular macaroni cheese and the Caribbean version is, of course, the spices. Here, I'm adding lots of ground yellow mustard, Cajun seasoning and nutmeg – the perfect partner for anything creamy or cheesy. This combination of spices adds a real kick, tons of extra flavour and brings out the tang of the strong cheese. Some people advocate using a mixture of Cheddar, Parmesan, Red Leicester and a hard blue cheese – so experiment at will.

Preheat the oven to 180°C/350°F/gas 4.

Cook the macaroni according to packet instructions.

Heat a large, heavy-based pan and melt the butter. Fry the garlic and bay leaves until the garlic is golden, then stir in the flour and continue to cook on a medium heat for another couple of minutes.

Gradually add the milk a little at a time, stirring it all together. Add the nutmeg, mustard powder, paprika and thyme and all but a handful of the cheese. Season well. Simmer until the sauce has thickened and the cheese melted.

Allow to cool slightly, then stir in the beaten eggs. Add the drained macaroni, mix together and transfer to an ovenproof dish. Sprinkle with the remaining cheese. Lay the sliced tomatoes on the top and bake for 30 minutes, or until the top is golden brown. Serve the macaroni cheese with plenty of hot peppersauce on the side.

EMMA'S GRILLED LEMON SOLE WITH MACE SERVES FOUR

PREP & COOK: 20 MINS

4 x 300g (11oz) whole
    lemon sole
a pinch of sea salt
1 lemon, thinly sliced

For the brown butter:
80g (3¼oz) lightly salted
    butter
2 blades mace
good ½ tsp freshly grated
    nutmeg
a sprinkling of capers
juice of 1 lemon
a sprinkling of freshly
    chopped parsley
sea salt and freshly
    ground black pepper

Lemon sole is not as tricky to prepare as you might think. Simply grilled and then combined with the subtle pepperiness of mace, the fresh sharpness of lemon and the creaminess of butter, it's delicious, and the flesh slides away from the ribby bones with ease.

Preheat the grill to medium, and line a roasting dish with greaseproof paper.

Place the fish, skin-side up, in the roasting dish. Sprinkle with a pinch of sea salt and arrange the lemon slices on top.

Grill under a medium heat for 8–10 minutes, until the fish is just cooked but easily comes away from the bone. Set aside to rest for 3 minutes while you make the brown butter.

In a large frying pan over a medium heat, heat the butter, mace and a pinch of salt. When the butter has melted and begins to bubble up and turn brown, throw in the nutmeg and capers and squeeze in the lemon juice. Stir in the chopped parsley, remove from the heat, discard the mace and season with salt and pepper. Arrange the sole on serving plates and pour the butter over the fish.

FLATTENED CHICKEN WITH SWISS CHARD GRATIN

PREP: 30 MINS
COOK: 30–35 MINS

1 x 1.5kg (3¼lb) chicken,
  deboned
2 white onions, thickly
  sliced into rings
1 head garlic, halved
  horizontally
1 lemon, halved horizontally
½ bunch thyme
olive oil, for drizzling
½ nutmeg, freshly grated
sea salt and freshly ground
  black pepper

For the Swiss chard gratin:
1.5kg (3¼lb) Swiss chard
  (spinach), leaves stripped
  from stalk, and stalk cut
  into 1cm (½in) strips
50g (2oz) butter, plus extra
  for greasing
6 garlic cloves, crushed with
  a pinch of salt until smooth
1 tbsp plain flour
250ml (8fl oz) milk
1 nutmeg
100g (3½oz) dried
  breadcrumbs
olive oil, for drizzling
sea salt and freshly ground
  black pepper

Ask your butcher to take the chicken off the bone for you. It cooks quickly and evenly like this. The Internet has loads of instructional videos if you want to do it yourself.

Preheat the oven to 200°C/400°F/gas 6. In a roasting tin, spread the onions, garlic and lemon halves in a single layer and scatter over the thyme sprigs. Season the chicken on both sides, then place, skin-side up, on the onion layer. Drizzle the skin generously with oil and grate the nutmeg over it. Bake for 40 minutes until the skin is golden and crisp and the flesh is cooked through (test by inserting a skewer into the flesh; if the juices run clear, the chicken is cooked). Cover and leave to rest. Leave the oven on.

Meanwhile, bring a large pan of salted water to the boil. Blanch the chard leaves until soft, about 1 minute. Remove from the pan with a slotted spoon and lay out on kitchen paper to drain and cool. In the same pan, boil the stalks until soft, about 10 minutes, then drain.

Butter a baking dish. In a large, heavy-based pan, melt the butter over a medium heat. When it begins to foam, add the garlic. After a minute or so, add the chard leaves and stalks, then sprinkle with the flour and cook, stirring, for 3 minutes. Slowly add the milk, still stirring, until you have a thick and glossy sauce. Grate in the nutmeg and season well with salt and pepper.

Transfer the chard mixture to the greased baking dish, sprinkle the breadcrumbs over it and drizzle with oil. Bake at 200°C/400°F/gas 6 for 20–25 minutes until golden. Remove the chicken from its tin, reserving the roasted onions and the resting juices. Slice the chicken, pour the resting juices over it and serve with the onions and the Swiss chard.

JERK-SPICED PORK CHOPS
WITH SWEET POTATO WEDGES AND THYME SALT

SERVES FOUR

**PREP: 20 MINS
+ 4 HRS MARINATING
COOK: 20–25 MINS**

4 x 150g (5oz) pork chops
lime wedges, to serve

For the marinade:
1 tbsp allspice berries
1 tbsp black peppercorns
½ tsp ground cinnamon
½ nutmeg, freshly grated
¼ bunch thyme, leaves picked
5 spring onions, roughly
   chopped
3 garlic cloves, roughly
   chopped
1 Scotch bonnet chilli, seeded
   and roughly chopped
1 tbsp dark brown sugar
2 tbsp dark soy sauce
juice of 1 lime
sea salt

For the roast sweet potatoes:
vegetable oil, for roasting
4 sweet potatoes, cut into
   eighths
2 tsp sea salt
5 thyme sprigs, leaves picked
   and roughly pounded in
   a pestle and mortar

Any leftover marinade can be stored in the fridge for a few days. You can use it with any grilled meat or fish, and it's great any time of the year.

In a pestle and mortar, pound the allspice and the peppercorns to a powder, then add to a food processor along with the cinnamon, nutmeg, thyme, spring onions, garlic and chilli. Blend to a paste, then stir in the sugar, soy sauce and lime juice. Pour the mixture into a large bowl, then add the pork and rub the marinade into the meat along with a little salt. Cover and leave to marinate for at least 4 hours, or overnight.

When you are ready to roast the potatoes, preheat the oven to 180°C/350°F/gas 4. Pour a very generous glug of oil into a shallow baking tray so that it's about ½cm (¼in) deep, then place in the oven for 5 minutes to heat up. When the oil's hot, add the sweet potatoes, toss quickly, and roast for 12–15 minutes, until golden and cooked through.

Meanwhile, heat a barbecue or griddle pan so that it's nice and hot, but not searing. Cook over a medium heat for 4 minutes each side. Leave to rest for a couple of minutes.

Remove the potatoes from the oven, stir 2 teaspoonfuls of salt through the bashed-up thyme and sprinkle over the hot potatoes. Serve with the pork chops, putting a wedge of lime on each plate.

NUTMEG & MACE QUICK FIXES

■ A blade of mace in cream of chicken soup or other creamy soups gives a hint of pungency.

■ Grate nutmeg over cheese on toast, cheese omelette or cauliflower cheese to add a spicy kick and extra depth of flavour.

■ Grating nutmeg over pasta dishes really peps up pesto or tomato sauces.

■ Freshly grated or ground nutmeg goes well with sweet potatoes and adds zip to carrots, spinach, broccoli or any other greens.

■ Nutmeg syrup – water, nutmeg, sugar and rum – is popular in Grenada. Drizzle over ice cream and fruit.

MIDDLE EASTERN NUTMEG BLEND

2 tsp ground nutmeg
2 tsp ground black pepper
2 tsp sweet paprika
1 tsp ground cumin
1 tsp ground cinnamon
½ tsp ground coriander
¼ tsp ground green cardamom seeds

Uses: add to lamb stew or sprinkle over roast lamb; season roasted root vegetables; rub dry on meat; sprinkle onto dips, such as hummus, or onto flatbreads, or use in dressing for salads.

EGGNOG

1 litre (1¾ pints) milk, preferably Jersey
100g (3½oz) sugar
6 egg yolks
100ml (3½fl oz) bourbon, dark rum or brandy

Eggnog spice blend:
½ tsp nutmeg, freshly grated, plus extra to serve
¼ tsp vanilla seeds, scraped from a vanilla pod
¼ tsp ground cinnamon
a pinch of ground allspice (optional)
a pinch of ground mace (optional)

Heat the milk and spices in a pan over a low heat for 5 minutes. Don't let the milk boil. In a clean bowl, whisk the sugar and egg yolks together until light in colour. Take the spice-infused milk off the heat and slowly whisk the sugar and egg into it, return to the heat and stir continuously. Once the mixture has thickened slightly (it won't be like custard but more the consistency of Baileys), stir in the rum and serve warm, or chilled, with some freshly grated nutmeg sprinkled on top.

NUTMEG & MACE RULES

Always grate whole nutmeg rather than using pre-ground, which rapidly loses its sparkle. Add nutmeg early to the dish to distribute flavour more evenly.

Nutmeg and cheese are partners in crime – goats', cows', sheeps' they all work really well together.

SLOW-COOKED PORK AND VEAL RAGÙ

PREP: 20 MINS
COOK: 1½–2 HRS

olive oil
1 celery heart, finely chopped
2 red onions, finely chopped
1 carrot, finely chopped
4 garlic cloves, finely chopped
a handful of sage leaves,
    chopped
3 bay leaves
400g (14oz) veal mince
400g (14oz) pork mince
120g (4½oz) pancetta slices,
    chopped
1 x 400g tin plum tomatoes,
    rinsed and drained
150ml (¼ pint) milk, plus
    extra if needed
peel of 1 lemon
3cm (1¼in) cinnamon stick
¾ nutmeg, freshly grated,
    plus extra to serve
sea salt and freshly ground
    black pepper

To serve:
spaghetti, pappardelle
    or penne
Parmesan

Add a good splash of olive oil to a large, heavy-based pan and place over a low heat. Gently fry the celery, onions, carrot, garlic and herbs with a pinch of salt for 10–15 minutes until soft and sweet. Remove the vegetables from the pan and set aside for a moment.

Carefully wipe the pan clean with kitchen paper, add another splash of oil and place over a high heat. Season the mince and add to the pan, along with the pancetta. Cook, stirring, for 8–10 minutes until the meat is caramelised and cooked through, then return the vegetables to the pan. Stir in the tomatoes, breaking them up a little with a wooden spoon. Add the milk, lemon peel, cinnamon and nutmeg. Bring to the boil, then turn the heat down to a simmer and leave the ragù to bubble away for 1½–2 hours, until the sauce is rich, thick and delicious. Add more milk if it looks like it's drying out. Serve with spaghetti, papardelle or penne and a good sprinkling of Parmesan. Finally grate a little extra nutmeg over the ragù before serving, if you wish.

PARMESAN BAKED POLENTA

WITH NUTMEG MEATBALLS AND RED WINE

PREP: 25 MINS
COOK: 40 MINS

For the polenta:
zest of 1 lemon
1 tsp table salt
200g (7oz) coarse polenta
15g (1oz) butter, plus
   extra for greasing
2 tbsp freshly grated
   Parmesan

For the sauce:
olive oil, for frying
3 garlic cloves, finely sliced
2 bay leaves
200ml (1/3 pint) red wine,
   ideally Chianti
2 x 400g tins plum tomatoes,
   rinsed and drained
sea salt and freshly ground
   black pepper

For the meatballs:
400g (14oz) pork mince
1 garlic clove, crushed
   with a pinch of salt
a pinch of dried chilli flakes
2/3 nutmeg, freshly grated
2 tbsp freshly grated
   Parmesan, plus extra
   to serve
olive oil
sea salt and freshly ground
   black pepper

Preheat the oven to 200°C/400°F/gas 6. Butter an oven dish.

In a very large pan, bring 1.5 litres (2½ pints) of water to the boil with the lemon zest and salt. Turn the heat down and very slowly add the polenta in a steady stream, whisking constantly to prevent lumps. Cook, stirring constantly, for 10 minutes. Transfer to the oven dish, dot the butter on top and sprinkle with 2 tablespoons of the Parmesan. Cover with foil and bake for 30 minutes, stirring once.

Meanwhile, to make the sauce, heat a little oil in a large, heavy-based pan, and very gently fry the garlic and bay leaves until the garlic begins to colour and becomes a bit sticky. Pour in the red wine, bring to the boil and reduce to a simmer for 5 minutes. Add the tomatoes, breaking them up with the back of a spoon, then pour in 250ml (8fl oz) water. Season well, reduce to a simmer and leave to bubble for 30 minutes.

While the polenta and the sauce are cooking, make the meatballs by combining the mince in a bowl with the garlic, chilli flakes, most of the nutmeg and 2 tbsp Parmesan. Season well. Heat a good glug of oil in a large frying pan, then fry a little of the mixture to test the seasoning, and adjust if necessary. Shape the mixture into about 20 balls with wet hands.

Heat a good glug of oil in a large frying pan, brown the meatballs in batches until golden, then transfer the meatballs to the red wine and tomato sauce and leave to simmer for at least 5 minutes.

Arrange the meatballs on top of the polenta and spoon the red wine and tomato sauce over them. Grate the remaining nutmeg over the top and return to the oven for another 10 minutes, until the meatballs are cooked through. Sprinkle with Parmesan, and serve.

BUTTERMILK PUDDINGS WITH NUTMEG-ROASTED PEACHES

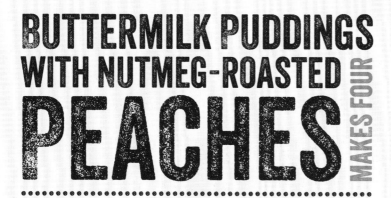

MAKES FOUR

PREP: 15 MINS
+ 2–3 HRS SETTING
COOK: 15 MINS

3 sheets (about 6g) gelatine
350ml (12fl oz) buttermilk
50g (2oz) sugar
250ml (8fl oz) double cream

For the roasted peaches:
4 firm peaches, halved
    and stoned
50g (2oz) butter
1 tbsp honey
¼ nutmeg

Buttermilk puddings are a wonderful old English dessert, a lot like panna cotta. Try to use gelatine sheets for this dish – they're far superior to powdered gelatine.

Soak the gelatine in cold water for a few minutes until soft, then squeeze out the excess water.

In a heavy-based pan, bring 100ml (3½fl oz) of the buttermilk to the boil with the sugar, and cook until the sugar has dissolved. Remove from the heat and stir in the gelatine until dissolved. Leave to cool, then whisk into the cream along with the remaining buttermilk. Pour into a shallow bowls or 4 small moulds and leave to set in the fridge for 2–3 hours, or overnight.

Preheat the oven to 180°C/350°F/gas 4. Place the peaches in a shallow roasting tin and dot with the butter. Drizzle with the honey, then grate the nutmeg over the peaches and roast for 15 minutes, or until the peaches are just tender and lightly browned. Leave to cool slightly.

Divide the buttermilk pudding between plates, then spoon the peach juices over the pudding and serve with the roasted peaches.

REALLY NUTMEGGY CUSTARD TART

PREP: 25 MINS + CHILLING
COOK: 40 MINS

For the pastry:
175g (6oz) plain flour
50g (2oz) icing sugar
a pinch of sea salt
100g (3½oz) butter, chilled
   and cut into cubes
2 egg yolks

For the custard:
500ml (18fl oz) double cream
10 egg yolks
75g (3oz) sugar
2 nutmegs

1 x 28cm (11in) tart tin
baking beans (or dried beans)

Custard tart is another old English dessert and perhaps the best of them all. This recipe really shows off nutmeg for the wonderful, exciting, yet comforting, spice that it is.

Sift the flour, sugar and salt into a mixing bowl, and combine. Rub in the butter with your fingertips (or combine in a food processor), until the mixture resembles coarse breadcrumbs. Add one of the egg yolks, and mix until the dough just comes together. Shape the dough into a ball, wrap in clingfilm and chill in the fridge for 1 hour.

Preheat the oven to 190°C/375°F/gas 5, and butter a 28cm (11in) tart tin.

Grate the pastry into the tart tin, and push it into the edges with your fingers. Prick the base a few times with a fork, then chill for 10 minutes. Line the chilled pastry with a piece of baking paper and fill with baking beans (or dried beans). Bake for 8–12 minutes, until the edges start to turn golden. Remove the paper and beans, then return the pastry to the oven for 5 minutes until golden. Remove from the oven and immediately brush the pastry with the remaining egg yolk. Leave to cool while you make the custard filling.

Turn the oven down to 140°C/275°F/gas 1. To make the custard, bring the cream to the boil in a heavy-based pan. In a bowl, whisk the egg yolks and sugar together, then add the hot cream and mix well. Pass the mixture through a sieve, then carefully pour the custard into the tart case, filling it right up to the brim. Grate the nutmegs generously over the top and bake for 30–40 minutes, or until the custard appears set but not too firm. Remove from the oven and allow to cool before serving.

CHERRY CLAFOUTIS
SERVES SIX

••

PREP: 25 MINS
COOK: 30 MINS

400g (14oz) cherries, stalks
    removed and flesh pierced
    a couple of times
80g (3¼oz) sugar, plus 2 tbsp
juice of 1 lemon
butter, for greasing
3 eggs, separated
40g (1½oz) plain flour
a pinch of table salt
250ml (8fl oz) milk
125g (4¾oz) crème fraîche
1 vanilla pod, seeds scraped
    and pod discarded
½ nutmeg, freshly grated
a generous splash of brandy

1 x 25cm (10in) baking dish

This French dessert doesn't traditionally include nutmeg, but its custardy batter seems the perfect home for nutmeg's fragrant sweetness. Take the stones out of the cherries if you wish, but it's a bit of a palaver, and the stones impart a subtle almond flavour. Although cherries are the classic fruit for this dish, pears, apples and blueberries are just as nice and a good excuse to eat clafoutis all year round.

Preheat the oven to 180°C/350°F/gas 4. Place the cherries in a bowl with the 2 tablespoons sugar and the lemon juice. Toss well and leave to sit for 20 minutes.

Lightly butter the baking dish and tip in the cherries.

In a clean bowl, beat the egg whites with half the sugar until you have glossy soft peaks. In a separate bowl, beat the egg yolks with the remaining sugar until light and creamy, then fold into the whites. Sift the flour and a pinch of salt into the bowl, then fold to combine. Stir well.

In another bowl, combine the milk, crème fraîche, vanilla seeds, nutmeg and brandy. Mix well, then stir into the egg mixture. Pour over the cherries.

Bake for 30 minutes until golden on top and slightly risen. Check to see if it's set and, if not, return to the oven for another 5 minutes or so. Serve warm.

PISTACHIO AND NUTMEG CAKE

SERVES TEN–TWELVE

**GLUTEN-FREE
PREP: 20 MINS
COOK: 45 MINS–1 HR**

150g (5oz) pistachios, finely
    ground, plus 75g (3oz)
    coarsely chopped
200g (7oz) ground almonds
220g (7½oz) soft brown sugar
120g (4½oz) butter, softened
1 tsp table salt
2 eggs, lightly beaten
250g (9oz) Greek-style
    yoghurt, plus extra to serve
1 tbsp freshly grated nutmeg
1 tsp baking powder

1 x 20cm (8in) round
    springform cake tin

This is a lovely yoghurty cake that I first had in Lebanon,
though I think it is actually originally from Syria. Try to find
really young, bright-green pistachios.

Preheat the oven to 180°C/350°F/gas 4. Line a 20cm (8in)
springform cake tin with baking paper.

In a bowl, combine the 150g (5oz) ground pistachios,
the almonds, sugar, butter and salt, and stir with a
wooden spoon until it all comes together. Spread half
the mixture evenly over the base of the cake tin.

Combine the remainder of the mixture with the eggs,
yoghurt, nutmeg and baking powder, and beat until
you have a smooth and creamy mixture. Pour into
the cake tin, then scatter with the 75g (3oz) chopped
pistachios. Bake for 45 minutes to an hour, until golden.
Leave to cool, then cut into slices and serve with
a dollop of yoghurt.

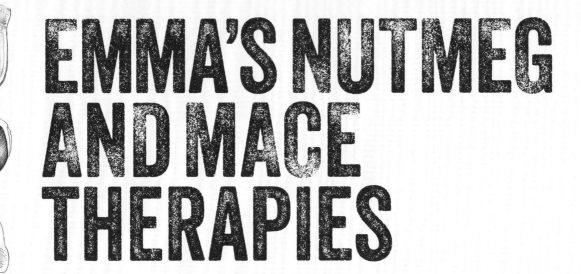

EMMA'S NUTMEG AND MACE THERAPIES

Both nutmeg and mace have been used in medicine since at least the 7th century. It was once believed that if a plant's shape resembled a part of the human body it could heal that part. As nutmeg has a similar oval shape to the brain, the ancient Greeks and Romans used it as a brain tonic. Indeed, today it's regarded as a potent brain booster, increasing blood circulation and improving concentration. The natural organic compound myristicin found in nutmeg has been shown to suppress an enzyme in the brain that contributes to Alzheimer's, and may help improve memory, so perhaps the old wives' tale has some truth to it after all.

According to 19th century Creole folklore, sprinkling nutmeg in a woman's left shoe each night at midnight would make her crazy with love! While this might be a little ambitious, the warming fragrance of nutmeg does give a feeling of relaxed wellbeing and can be used to relieve stress; indeed, in homeopathy it is used to treat anxiety and depression.

THE STORY OF NUTMEG & MACE

Nutmeg has the most bloody history of all the spices. It is indigenous to the Banda islands in Indonesia, which was the only source until the early 19th century. The islands see-sawed between Portuguese, Dutch and, briefly, British rule. Under the dominion of the Dutch East India Company in the early 17th century, the islands were the stage for a bloody war, leading to the massacre and enslavement of the Bandan people. Export of nutmeg trees was banned; every nutmeg was drenched in lime to prevent germination and the death

penalty enforced for stealing, growing or selling nutmegs outside the island. When some of the locals broke these 'rules', there was systematic quartering and beheading of every Bandanese male over 15 years of age. In 15 years, the population of the Banda Islands was reduced from 15,000 to just 600.

During British control of the spice trade from 1796 to 1802, nutmeg trees were transplanted to other British colonies, including Grenada. This island now produces much of the world's nutmeg

and its importance is celebrated with a nutmeg symbol on the national flag.

In the past, as with many of our spices, nutmeg and mace were the preserve of the wealthy; one small bag was said to provide financial independence for life. In Elizabethan times the price rocketed as word spread that nutmeg would ward off the plague. And in the Victorian era, the affectation of carrying elaborate graters was a mark of wealth: it's said that Dickens carried a monogrammed grater in his waistcoat pocket.

A NOTE OF A WARNING:

While myristicin is a potential healer, it is also both toxic and narcotic if taken in large quantities – so beware! The old apothecaries were cautious about its benefits: 'One nut is good for you, the second will do you harm, the third will kill you'. While this is not strictly true (although there are cases of death by nutmeg), large doses of more than 6 tablespoons a day can be dangerously intoxicating. In his autobiography, Malcolm X wrote of US prisoners smoking the spice during his time in jail, and William S. Burroughs talked of its hallucinogenic effects, with side effects of headache and nausea. Hallucinogen poisoning, where the myrisiticin acts as a deliriant, can induce convulsions, palpitations, nausea and dehydration.

MEDICINAL USES

■ Nutmeg oil is anti-inflammatory and can be used to treat joint and muscle pains by rubbing it in to the affected area. Mixed with almond oil, it can also relieve rheumatic pain.

■ A few drops of nutmeg oil mixed with honey can relieve flatulence, nausea and gastroenteritis.

■ In holistic medicine, nutmeg oil is considered a great detoxifier for the liver and kidneys.

■ The eugenol compound found in nutmeg may benefit the heart by lowering blood pressure and helping circulation.

■ Nutmeg's antibacterial properties are effective in treating bad breath and toothache.

■ If you have a cold, laying a cloth covered with a paste of nutmeg powder, flour and water across the chest can ease congestion.

■ To soothe acne, spread a paste of 2–3 nutmegs ground and mixed with milk over the affected area, and leave for 2 hours. Remove with warm water and splash with cold water to close the pores.

■ Grated nutmeg mixed with lard is reputed to be an excellent ointment for haemorrhoids!

'SLEEPYTIME' NUTMEG BALLS

In small amounts the compound myristicin, found in nutmeg, can cause drowsiness and induce sleep, especially as its effects have a delayed onset; meaning it's great for people who tend to wake after a few hours and have problems falling back to sleep. Almonds contain magnesium, which helps us to relax, tryptophan and an essential amino acid which some studies show helps to reduce the time it takes to fall asleep.

½ tsp nutmeg, freshly ground
1 tbsp ground almonds
honey

Mix the ground nutmeg with the ground almonds along with enough honey to make into a stiff paste. Form into pea-sized balls and store in the fridge.

Take two of the balls before bed.

NOTE: do not take any more than two balls or add any more nutmeg to the recipe. Whilst myristicin helps induce sleep in small amounts, in very large amounts it can cause headaches and hallucinations.

For those who don't fancy the balls, make a simple 'Sleepytime' drink by stirring ¼ teaspoon freshly grated nutmeg into warm milk or almond milk for extra sleep-inducing power. Heat until just about to boil, add honey to taste and drink before bed.

NUTMEG PERFUME OIL

nutmeg oil
allspice/ pimento oil
orange or bergamot oil
sweet almond oil

Nutmeg is used in many classic perfumes, including Chanel no. 5. It creates an earthy, gently spiced undertone. Many perfumes contain alcohol, which helps a fragrance release its aroma more quickly (as it's more volatile). Mixing a perfume with oil instead helps it to stay on the skin for longer. I use perfume oils instead of alcohol-based ones as I love the way they cling to your clothes and skin for days. They smell far more natural and never overpower like some perfumes can.

'UNDER THE COUNTER'

'Under the counter' is the aptly named aphrodisiac drink widely sold from under counters all over Grenada. It is a rum-based moonshine infused with spices and an interesting bark, the name of which translates as 'hard wood'.

1 x 750 ml bottle of white rum (use Grenadian rum at your peril – drinking it makes you feel as though you have run into a wall headfirst)

1 nutmeg
2 cinnamon sticks
3 bay leaves
½ tsp cloves
½ tsp allspice berries

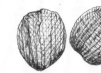

Bash the nutmeg into chunks, break the
cinnamon quills, and add all the spices into
the rum. Leave to infuse for at least 4 weeks,
preferably more.

'NUTMEG DANGER'
'Under the Counter' works wonderfully well in
Stevie's rum punch, or as we have named it
'Nutmeg Danger' because it's so easy to drink.

3 bottles of sparkling wine/prosecco/Champagne
1 bottle of 'under the counter' or rum
1 x 750ml bottle of cognac or brandy
1 x 500ml bottle of whisky or bourbon
juice of 10 lemons
450g sugar
20 party friends and some jammin' music

Muddle all the ingredients together and drink
over ice at your leisure/peril.

CLOVES
ZANZIBAR
3

'FAR FROM SIMPLY BEING THE SPICE THAT MOST REMINDS US OF CHRISTMAS, MINCE PIES, MULLED WINE AND POMANDERS, CLOVES ARE DARK, MUSKY AND POSSESSIVE OF A POWERFULLY NUMBING FLAVOUR THAT IS AS MYSTERIOUS AS THE EXOTIC ARABIC CULTURE IN ZANZIBAR'

For most of us, cloves mean Christmas, but in many countries – particularly Zanzibar, parts of India and much of the Caribbean – a pot of rice just isn't a pot of rice without a few cloves chucked in – they bring a wonderful clean flavour to the dish.

For me the taste of cloves has much to do with the effect it has on your mouth. Suck on a clove and you'll soon see that it acts as a surprisingly strong local anaesthetic. But the taste that comes with this sensation is something special. There's a little menthol, a bit of anise, something like nutmeg, but stronger, and a hint of cinnamon. It's a surprisingly wonderful flavour that can be used in almost any dish. I chuck cloves in stews, coffee, curry and always in rice. I rarely bother to grind them so I throw them in and leave them for people to have a bit of a chew on; they can always fish them out if they want. Just take care as using more than a few cloves in delicate dishes can overpower the other ingredients.

Cloves are insanely pretty when they grow – like bright pink and green sweeties. They are the flowers of the evergreen *Syzygium aromaticum*, which grows to an enormous height that you have to scale to harvest. The best cloves come from the buds rather than the flowers. If they're picked after flowering, they won't have the little bud on the top and the flavour won't be as vibrant and clean. After just three days in the sun, you have the little brown 'nails' (as in the French *clou*) that look just like the cloves we get at home. I wasn't the best clove harvester – I'm not very good at climbing trees – and seeing how hard it is gave me a new respect for this little brown spice.

Each spice has its own character, which is determined by several factors – its flavour, the foods it's used in, the countries in which it grows and the history of its cultivation and distribution; never is this more evident than in the well known clove. Far from simply being the spice that most reminds us of Christmas, mince pies, mulled wine and pomanders, cloves are, in my eyes, dark, musky and possessive of a powerfully numbing flavour that is as mysterious as the exotic Arabic culture in Zanzibar.

The history of the clove is as dark as its flavour; in Zanzibar we learned about the East African slave trade and its massive role in the cultivation and worldwide distribution of the spice. It's a sad subject and one that really moved me. However, the Zanzibarians I spoke to maintain a level, matter-of-fact stance on their history and, curiously, their strength as a people seems to mirror the phenomenal medicinal strength of the cloves on which the island thrives. From now on, whenever I use cloves, I'll think of strength, and the incredible people we met.

Buy brown or red cloves rather than the black ones – the darker cloves have been sun-dried for longer and are older and less aromatic. Squeeze the buds to see if they are fresh; they should leave a trace of oil on your fingers. Cloves will keep for up to a year if kept in a cool, dark place. Pre-ground cloves keep their flavour well because of their high oil content, and cloves are one of the few spices that are acceptable to buy this way. Don't be heavy-handed when adding cloves to your cooking; they are VERY powerful and pungent, and only a small amount is needed in most recipes.

EMMA'S SIMPLE SLOW-COOKED
TOMATO AND BASIL SAUCE

SERVES FOUR

PREP: 20 MINS
COOK: 20 MINS

olive oil
1 red onion, diced
3 garlic cloves, finely chopped
3 x 400g tins plum tomatoes,
    drained, rinsed and roughly
    chopped
½ tsp ground cloves
¼ tsp nutmeg, freshly ground,
    plus extra, to serve
a good handful of basil leaves
sea salt and freshly ground
    black pepper, to serve

To serve:
500g dried pasta,
    such as rigatoni
Parmesan

Basil and cloves share a chemical compound and
complement each other well. When the two are combined,
the result is a wonderful, unexpected flavour – rather like
basil but stronger, more potent and with more depth.
This simply cooked tomato sauce served with pasta is
all you need to create a satisfying and interesting meal.

Heat a good glug of oil in a large, heavy-based pan,
and gently fry the onion for 10–15 minutes until soft
and translucent. Add the garlic and cook until golden,
then add the tomatoes, spices, pepper and salt. Simmer
for 20 minutes, or longer if you have the time.

Meanwhile, cook the pasta according to packet
instructions. Drain and divide between 4 serving plates.

Tear the basil into the sauce, spoon the sauce over the
pasta, grate some Parmesan over the top and add an
extra pinch of ground cloves before serving.

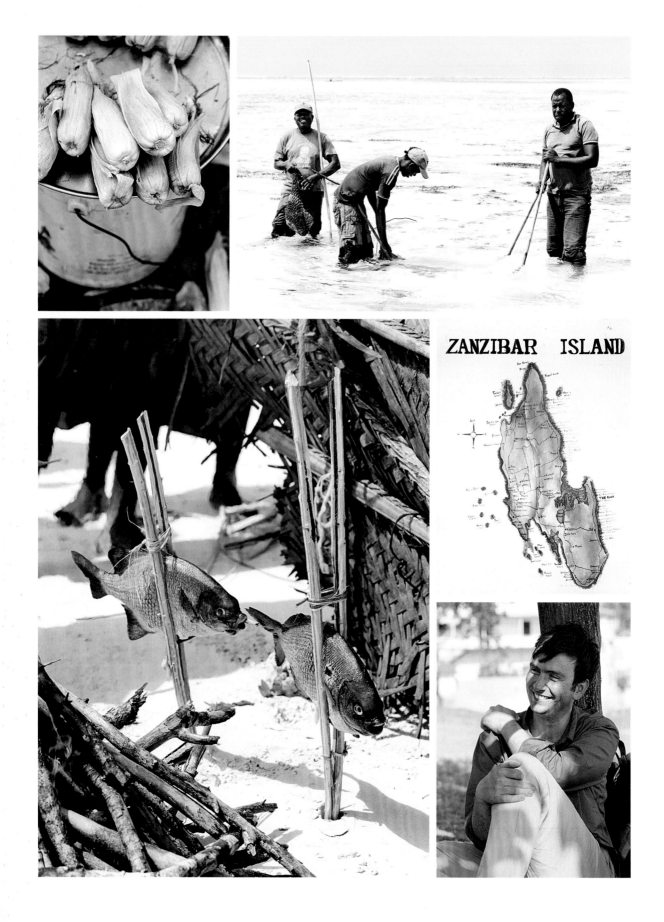

ZANZIBAR ISLAND

MY FAVOURITE KEDGEREE

SERVES FOUR

PREP: 10 MINS
COOK: 35 MINS

500ml (18fl oz) milk
3 bay leaves
a handful of parsley stalks
20 black peppercorns
15 whole cloves, plus ½ tsp
    ground cloves
450g (1lb) undyed smoked
    haddock fillet
150g (5oz) basmati rice,
    soaked for 1 hour in
    cold water
50g (2oz) butter
1 white onion, chopped
½ tsp turmeric
½ tsp ground coriander
sea salt and freshly ground
    black pepper

To serve:
4 hard-boiled eggs, peeled
    and halved
a handful of coriander leaves,
crème fraîche (optional)

My wife makes wonderful kedgeree. Great as a breakfast, lunch or dinner, this version turns out lovely and fluffy and is not as rich as some more cheffy, buttery versions with cream and poached eggs.

In a large, wide pan, bring the milk, 100ml (3½fl oz) water, bay leaves, parsley stalks, peppercorns. a pinch of salt and whole cloves to the boil. Turn the heat down to a simmer, add the fish, and as soon as it begins to simmer again, take the pan off the heat. Leave the fish in the milk for 5 minutes, then drain (reserving the liquid and discarding the herbs and spices). Flake the haddock on to a plate, cover with clingfilm and set to one side.

Drain the rice and put into a large pan. Pour the haddock cooking liquid over the rice so that it comes 2cm (¾in) above it. Taste and add a little salt if necessary. Bring to the boil and cook for 5 minutes uncovered, then turn down to a simmer and cook for another 5 minutes. Take off the heat, put a lid on the pan and leave to sit, covered, for 10 minutes.

Meanwhile, melt the butter in a large, heavy-based pan and add the onion. Slowly cook until it begins to colour slightly, then add the ground cloves, turmeric and ground coriander. Continue to slowly cook for 10–15 minutes until the onions are soft and sweet. Spoon in the rice and gently combine with the onions. Carefully fold in the haddock, then transfer to a serving platter or plates. Top with the boiled eggs, scatter with the coriander and add a dollop of crème fraîche if you want.

CHICKEN KEBABS
WITH CHOPPED SALAD AND TAHINI SAUCE

PREP & COOK: 20 MINS

For the tahini sauce:
½ garlic clove, crushed
    with a pinch of salt
juice of 2 lemons
3 tbsp tahini
olive oil

For the kebabs and salad:
½ tsp Szechuan peppercorns,
    toasted
1 star anise
7 whole cloves
1cm (½in) cinnamon stick
3 black peppercorns
¼ tsp fennel seeds
4 chicken thighs, boned
½ cucumber, roughly chopped
1 tomato, roughly chopped
the seeds from ¼ pomegranate
juice of ½ lemon
olive oil
sea salt and freshly ground
    black pepper

To serve:
4 flatbreads

Tahini paste, made with ground sesame seeds, is a versatile ingredient. You can use it with meat, fish or vegetables, but try to buy a tahini that's quite light in colour as the darker ones tend to taste like peanut butter. These lovely little kebabs work well with lamb, or even livers, too.

Make your tahini sauce by combining the garlic, lemon juice, tahini and a good glug of oil in a bowl. Pour in cold water, stirring constantly, until you have a mixture that resembles double cream. Taste it – it should be zingy and quite acidic, full-flavoured enough to work as a condiment.

Heat a griddle pan until searingly hot.

In a pestle and mortar, grind the spices vigorously until you have a coarse powder. Transfer to a large bowl, add the chicken and rub the spices into the meat, season with salt and grill for 8 minutes on both sides until cooked through. Cut into thick slices and keep warm.

Combine the cucumber, tomato and pomegranate in a bowl. Season well, squeeze the lemon juice over the salad and drizzle with a little oil. Toss well.

Warm your flatbreads. Split them open and stuff each one with the salad, followed by the chicken and a generous drizzle of tahini sauce.

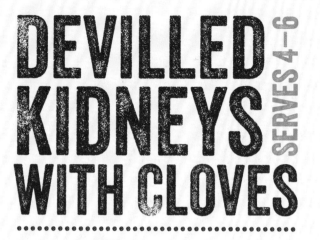

DEVILLED KIDNEYS WITH CLOVES

SERVES 4–6

PREP & COOK: 10 MINS

½ tsp ground cloves
2 tsp mustard powder
½ tsp cayenne pepper,
  or a little extra if you're
  very devillish
2 tsp plain flour
8 kidneys, trimmed and
  cut in half lengthways
15g (½oz) butter
sherry vinegar
sea salt and freshly ground
  black pepper

To serve:
toasted sourdough bread
1 tbsp parsley, roughly
  chopped

Kidneys aren't to everyone's taste, but I love them. The best ones come from calves, though these can be quite expensive so I generally go for lambs' kidneys, which are also delicious. To trim them simply remove the outer membrane and cut out the gristly core.

Combine the dry ingredients in a bowl and season well. Add the kidneys and roll them in the mixture until well covered.

Melt the butter in a heavy-based pan over a medium-high heat and when it begins to froth, add the kidneys and cook for about 3 minutes each side, until they begin to colour. Take off the heat, stir in a couple of dessertspoonfuls of sherry vinegar, spoon the kidneys over the toasts and pour the warm vinegary butter over them. Scatter with a little chopped parsley, and serve.

EMMA'S BUTTERY CLOVE CINNAMON AND BLACK PEPPER RICE

SERVES SIX

PREP & COOK: 25 MINS

a generous knob of butter
1 cinnamon stick
½ tsp whole cloves
½ tsp black peppercorns
300g (11oz) basmati rice
½ tsp table salt
toasted sliced almonds or
    cashew nuts, to sprinkle

Velvety and fragrant, the spices here are subtle, not overwhelming, but nonetheless evident as rice takes on flavour really well. This rice dish is the perfect accompaniment to fish or curry, adding a unique flavour to any meal.

In a heavy-based pan (with a lid), melt the butter over a medium heat, and fry the spices for 1 minute.

Add the dry rice and stir to coat. Pour in 400ml (14fl oz) water and add the salt. Put the lid on the pan and simmer for 20 minutes or until the rice is cooked – but don't stir or it'll be impossible to pick out the spices later. When the rice is cooked, the whole spices will have risen to the surface and you can pick them out before you fluff up the rice with a fork. Sprinkle with toasted almonds or cashew nuts.

CLOVE RULES

Cloves can very easily overpower a dish so they work best when they can be easily removed after they've imparted their flavour.

Cloves are so versatile that it's worth keeping some of the ground spice to hand to add to curry powders, spice rubs or desserts.

WARNING use with caution, a ¼ teaspoon can overwhelm most flavours.

STORAGE

Whole: store for about a year

Ground: will keep for about 6 months

CLOVE QUICK FIXES

■ Add a pinch of ground cloves to red meat dishes to bring out the meat flavour; add a pinch to gravy for a richer sauce

■ Place an onion studded with cloves into the body of a duck before roasting

■ Stud a shallot with cloves to flavour béchamel – simmer in the milk before adding the milk to the roux

■ If you make your own marmalade, cloves are a fantastic addition

CLOVE SPICE BLEND

¼ tsp ground cloves
¼ tsp ground nutmeg
½ tsp ground black pepper
1 tsp ground cinnamon
2 tbsp sugar
a pinch of salt

Uses: an exotic hot blend to sprinkle on fruit or make into a syrup to pour over waffles or add to winter puddings

GRILLED MACKEREL WITH HOT FRUIT AND CLOVE SALSA

SERVES FOUR

PREP & COOK: 20 MINS

¼ pineapple, chopped into small chunks
1 mango, preferably Alfonso, chopped into small chunks
1 large tomato, chopped into small chunks
a few gratings of nutmeg
2 tsp ground cloves
1 tbsp sugar
juice of 1 lemon, plus wedges to serve
4 mackerel, cleaned and gutted
olive oil
1 tsp ground allspice
½ tsp ground cinnamon
sea salt and freshly ground black pepper

This simple, fresh salsa brings a bit of zing to lovely grilled mackerel. Perhaps my favourite fish, mackerel is super cheap, but it needs to be really fresh for cooking.

In a bowl, toss the pineapple, mango and tomato with the nutmeg and 1 teaspoon of the ground cloves. Put to one side.

Put the sugar and 2 tablespoons of water into a pan over a medium heat for about 1 minute until you have a syrup. Add the fruit, stir once and take off the heat. Stir in the lemon juice and keep warm.

Heat a griddle pan or barbecue until very hot (or preheat the grill to high). Season the mackerel, rub them in a little oil and sprinkle with the allspice, cinnamon and the remaining teaspoon of ground cloves. Grill for 2–3 minutes on each side until golden and cooked through. Divide the mackerel between 4 serving plates and serve with the fruit salad and a wedge of lemon on each plate.

MY GRANDDAD'S STICKY CLOVE
BOURBON HAM

PREP: 5 MINS
COOK: 45 MINS

1 x 3kg (7lb) cooked ham
  on the bone, cooled
about 20 whole cloves
4 tbsp orange marmalade
4 tbsp honey
4 tbsp Dijon mustard
100ml (3½fl oz) bourbon

Glazed ham studded with cloves is a traditional favourite recipe. The addition of bourbon to the classic Christmas ham adds another level of flavour. It's a great dish to cook at any time, so why wait for Christmas? It tastes just as good cold for lunch and is ideal for a picnic or a big party.

Preheat the oven to 160°C/325°F/gas 3.

Cut the rind off the cooked ham, leaving the fat, and place the ham in a roasting tin. With a sharp knife, score the fat in a diamond pattern, taking care not to cut through to the meat, and stick a clove into the centre of each diamond.

In a bowl, mix the marmalade, honey, mustard and bourbon together and, using a pastry brush or palette knife, spread the ham with a third of the glaze. Bake for 15 minutes, then take the ham out of the oven and spread with another third of the glaze. Return the ham to the oven for another 15 minutes, then spread with the remaining glaze and return to the oven for a final 15 minutes.

Remove the ham from the oven and let it rest for 15 minutes, before slicing.

MULLED WINE OXTAIL STEW

PREP: 20 MINS
COOK: 3 HRS

For the mulled wine:
1 cinnamon stick
1 star anise
10 whole cloves
3 bay leaves
10–12 gratings nutmeg
whole peel of 1 orange
1–3 tbsp sugar
2 celery sticks
2 white onions, halved
3 carrots, halved
1 head of garlic, halved
   horizontally
1 bottle of red wine
1.5kg (3¼lb) oxtail pieces,
   preferably cut from the
   larger end
3 tbsp plain flour, seasoned
   with salt and pepper

For the salad:
2 fennel bulbs, tough outer
   layer discarded and the
   rest thinly sliced
2 oranges, peeled, pithed
   and cut into half moons
1 tbsp black olives, roughly
   chopped
½ small red onion, thinly
   sliced
a handful of parsley leaves,
   roughly chopped
olive oil
red wine vinegar
sea salt and freshly ground
   black pepper

This is a surprising dish. I was quite delighted when I was drinking mulled wine and suddenly realised it would make a wonderful stew. This recipe works with other pieces of stewing beef but tail has a wonderfully comforting, gelatinous quality to it that I love.

Preheat the oven to 150°C/300°F/gas 2.

Place the cinnamon, star anise, cloves, bay leaves, nutmeg, orange peel, sugar and vegetables in a large pan and pour in the wine. Bring to the boil, then turn down to a simmer and cook for 10 minutes.

Toss the oxtail pieces in the seasoned flour so they're completely covered. Shake off the excess. Heat a good glug of oil in a heavy-based pan (with a lid) and brown them on all sides. When they're nice and golden, pour in the mulled wine mixture. Season well. Put the lid on and bake for 3 hours, or until the meat falls easily from the bone – sometimes it takes a bit longer, but it will happen eventually.

When the oxtail is ready, combine all the fresh salad ingredients in a bowl, season well with salt and pepper, add good splashes of oil and vinegar and toss well to combine.

Remove the oxtail from the pan. Skim off any excess fat from the sauce and reduce it a little. Return the oxtail to the sauce and serve with the salad either on top or on the side.

CHAIRMAN MAO'S RED
PORK BELLY

SERVES SIX

PREP: 10 MINS
COOK: 3 HRS

1.5kg (3¼lb) pork belly, cut
   into 3cm (1¼in) chunks
ground nut oil
3 red onions, finely sliced
20g (¾oz) ginger, peeled
   and sliced
4 garlic cloves, roughly
   chopped
1 tbsp ground coriander
1 star anise
1 tbsp ground cloves
3 dried red chillies
250ml (8fl oz) rice wine
   vinegar
200g (7oz) sugar
sea salt

To serve:
steamed rice
a few coriander leaves

Preheat the oven to 150°C/300°F/gas 2.

Season the pork with salt. In a large, heavy-based pan (with a lid), heat some oil and brown the pork on all sides, then remove from the pan and keep warm.

Pour off a little oil from the pan if necessary, then add the onions, ginger, garlic, ground coriander, star anise, cloves and red chillies and cook over a medium heat until the onions are soft (about 10 minutes). Return the pork to the pan, pour in the vinegar and add the sugar and 250ml (8fl oz) cold water. Cover with the lid and slow-cook in the oven for 3 hours, until soft and tender. Sprinkle over the coriander leaves and serve with steamed rice.

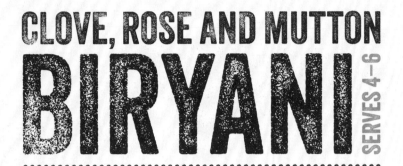

CLOVE, ROSE AND MUTTON
BIRYANI

SERVES 4–6

PREP: 20 MINS
COOK: 4½ HOURS

8 garlic cloves
3cm (1¼in) piece ginger
2 tsp sea salt
olive oil
1 x 2kg (4½lb) lamb or mutton
   shoulder, bone out, trimmed
   of excess fat and cut into
   5cm (2in) chunks
2 onions, chopped
1 x 400g tin plum tomatoes,
   drained, rinsed and roughly
   chopped
1 tbsp red wine vinegar
2 heaped tbsp natural yoghurt
2 tbsp ground almonds
500g (1¼lb) basmati rice,
   soaked for 1 hour
a small pinch of saffron
   threads, soaked in 50ml
   (2fl oz) boiling water
400g (14oz) plain flour (or
   more, depending on the
   width of your oven dish),
   plus extra for dusting
sea salt and freshly ground
   black pepper
a handful of fresh rose petals,
   to decorate
pomegranate seeds and
   coriander leaves, to serve

Ingredients continue overleaf

You should be able to find dried rose petals in Middle Eastern stores or online, but if you can't, just leave them out. It is nice to finish this dish with fresh rose petals or other edible flowers, but only if they've been grown organically or specially for eating.

In a pestle and mortar, bash the garlic and ginger together with the salt until you have a rough paste. Put to one side.

Prepare the spice mix (see overleaf) by placing all the whole spices, except for the cinnamon, in a food processor, spice grinder or pestle and mortar and grind everything to a fine powder. Stir in the turmeric and chilli powder. Put to one side.

Heat some oil in a large, heavy-based pan (with a lid). Season the lamb and brown in the pan until golden on all sides. Remove from the pan and set aside. Add the onions to the pan and stir well, picking up the sticky bits from the bottom of the pan. When the onions begin to soften, stir in the garlic and ginger mix and another dash of oil if necessary, and cook for 2 minutes before adding the spice mix and the cinnamon stick. Continue to cook for another 5 minutes, until the onions are soft and the spices smell wonderful.

Return the lamb to the pan and add the tomatoes, vinegar, yoghurt and ground almonds, stirring to pick up the spices stuck on the bottom of the pan. Taste for seasoning, and add enough cold water to easily cover the lamb. Bring to the boil, put the lid on the pan and leave to simmer for 4 hours, until the lamb is tender.

Recipe continues overleaf

For the spice mix:
1 tbsp whole cloves
2 tbsp cumin seeds, toasted
1½ tbsp coriander seeds, toasted
1 tbsp black peppercorns
1½ tsp fennel seeds
1 tsp fenugreek
5 green and 5 black cardamom
   pods (or 10 green if you can't
   find black), seeds to be used
   and shells discarded
1 tbsp dried rose petals (optional)
½ tsp turmeric
¼ tsp chilli powder
4cm (1½in) cinnamon stick

Recipe continued

Preheat the oven to 180°C/350°F/gas 4. Drain the rice and cover with boiling water and a pinch of salt. Boil for 4 minutes, then drain and leave to steam in its pan with a lid.

Generously cover the bottom of a large, ovenproof dish with half the lamb mixture. Cover with half the rice, then the remaining lamb and, finally, the remaining rice. Pour in the saffron water.

Place the flour in a large bowl, and work in enough cold water to make a stiff dough. Knead until you have a smooth dough, then roll out with a floured rolling pin, and use to cover the dish. Pinch the sides to make sure it stays tight. Bake for 20–25 minutes, until the bread dough has turned golden.

Serve the biryani with the bread crust intact for your guests to break into. Arrange the rose petals, coriander leaves and pomegranate seeds on the side to sprinkle over the rice.

SWEET MILK RICE AND CLOVE TARTS

**PREP: 10 MINS
+ 20 MINS CHILLING
COOK: 1 HR 10 MINS**

For the pastry:
200g (7oz) plain flour, sifted,
    plus extra for dusting
a pinch of table salt
150g (5oz) butter, chilled
    and cut into small cubes,
    plus extra for greasing
2 egg yolks, beaten

For the filling:
400ml (14fl oz) milk
10 whole cloves
150g (5oz) risotto rice, rinsed
whole peel of 1 orange
a pinch of sea salt
100g (3½oz) sugar
50g (2oz) butter
2 egg yolks

For the topping:
icing sugar, sifted
½ tsp ground cloves,
    to decorate

1 x 12-hole muffin tray

In the *gran caffés* of Florence these rice pastries (*budini al riso*) are one of my favourite accompaniments to coffee. They are easy to make and the scent of the cloves permeates everything beautifully.

Put the flour and salt into a large bowl and rub in the butter with your fingertips (or combine the ingredients in a food processor) until the mixture resembles coarse breadcrumbs. Gradually fold in the beaten egg yolks until the dough just comes together, then shape into a ball. Wrap in clingfilm and chill in the fridge for 20 minutes.

To make the filling, bring the milk to the boil with the cloves, then add the rice, orange peel (give it a twist to release the oils) and a pinch of salt. Cook, stirring occasionally, until the rice is fully cooked (about 45 minutes), then take off the heat and stir in the sugar, butter and egg yolks. Leave to cool.

Preheat the oven to 180°C/350°F/gas 4. Butter a 12-hole muffin tray. Coarsely grate a little pastry into each hole and press the pastry into the sides with your fingers until each hole is neatly filled with a good layer of pastry.

Taste the rice pudding and add more sugar or salt if necessary. Divide the cooled rice pudding between the pastry cases, filling each one to the brim.

Bake for 15 minutes until the tarts begin to turn golden, then cover loosely with foil and return to the oven for another 10 minutes. Remove and leave to cool before lightly dusting with icing sugar and the ground cloves.

ORANGE MARMALADE AND CLOVE TART

SERVES TWELVE

PREP: 20 MINS
+ 1 HR CHILLING
COOK: 20 MINS

For the pastry:
175g (6oz) plain flour
50g (2oz) icing sugar
a pinch of sea salt
100g (3½oz) butter, chilled
   and cut into cubes
2 egg yolks

For the filling:
160g (5½oz) sugar
juice of 6 oranges, plus
   zest of 3
4 tbsp good-quality orange
   marmalade
20 whole cloves, plus a
   pinch of ground cloves
5 eggs and 6 egg yolks,
   beaten together
200g (7oz) butter, cut
   into small cubes

1 x 28cm (11in)
   loose-bottomed tart tin

To serve:
crème frâiche

This is an interesting variation on the classic lemon tart. A dark marmalade will carry the flavour better than a mild, light one.

Sift the flour, sugar and salt into a mixing bowl, and combine. Rub in the butter with your fingertips (or combine in a food processor), until the mixture resembles coarse breadcrumbs. Add one of the egg yolks, and mix until the dough just comes together. Shape the dough into a ball, wrap in clingfilm and chill in the fridge for 1 hour.

Preheat the oven to 190°C/375°F/gas 5, and butter a 28cm (11in) tart tin.

Coarsely grate the pastry into the tin, pressing it into the edges with your fingers. Prick the base several times with a fork, then place in the freezer for 15 minutes to chill. Then transfer to the hot oven and bake for 15 minutes until golden. Remove and leave to cool.

Turn the oven down to 150°C/300°F/gas 2. For the filling, put the sugar, orange juice, zest, marmalade and cloves in a heavy-based pan, bring to the boil and cook until the sugar has dissolved. Turn the heat down very low and whisk in the eggs and yolks. Whisk until the mixture starts to thicken, then stir in the butter, making sure you scrape the bottom of the pan each time. Continue to cook, stirring over a low heat. When the mixture looks like thick custard and coats the back of a spoon, take it off the heat and leave to cool a little. Give it a whisk, then strain through a sieve to remove the cloves. Pour the mixture into the baked tart shell and sprinkle with the ground cloves. Bake in the oven for 20 minutes until just set, then leave to cool. Serve with crème fraîche.

CLOVES
SWEET
THINGS

APPLE TARTE FINE WITH CLOVE BUTTERSCOTCH

PREP & COOK: 20–25 MINS

1 x 375g puff pastry
flour, for dusting work surface
40g (1½oz) butter
40g (1½oz) light brown sugar
1 tsp ground cloves
squeeze of lemon juice
50ml (2fl oz) double cream
4–5 Golden Delicious apples,
  peeled, cored and thinly
  sliced

To serve:
crème fraîche, yoghurt
  or vanilla ice cream

This is based on the traditional French *tarte fine* –
a brilliant dessert that is so simple to make, especially
if you cheat and use ready-made puff pastry. Even though
this tart is very thin and delicate, it's pretty rich and is best
served with crème fraîche or yoghurt to cut the sweetness
a bit. Apple and cloves are a great English flavour
combination and when I eat this, it always reminds
me of the baked apples with sultanas and mixed spice
that my mum used to make.

Preheat the oven to 200°C/400°F/gas 6. Line a large
baking tray with baking paper.

On a lightly floured surface, roll out the pastry in a long,
4mm-thick rectangle. Place on the baking tray and prick
with a fork several times to stop it puffing up. Place in the
fridge to chill.

Make the butterscotch by combining the butter, sugar
and cloves in a heavy-based pan. Cook over a medium
heat until the sugar has dissolved, then take off the
heat and add the lemon juice. Stir in the cream.

Arrange the apple slices tightly, but neatly, on
the chilled pastry, overlapping them, and leaving a
½cm (¼in) border around the edge. Brush the apples
generously with the butterscotch mixture and bake for
10–15 minutes until the pastry is cooked and the apples
are tender. Serve with any leftover warm butterscotch
and crème fraîche, yoghurt or vanilla ice cream.

EMMA'S POLENTA CAKE
WITH CLOVE AND ORANGE CARAMEL

PREP: 45 MINS
COOK: 1 HR

5 oranges: 2 peeled and thinly
    sliced, 2 chopped, and
    1 juiced
120g (4½oz) butter, at room
    temperature, plus extra
    for greasing tin
280g (10oz) sugar
2 eggs
1 level tbsp ground cloves
1 tsp baking powder
30g (1¼oz) plain flour, sifted
140g (4¾oz) polenta
120g (4½oz) ground almonds

1 x 20cm (8in) round cake tin

To serve:
crème fraîche or yoghurt

Dark and exotic, this cake evokes memories of the
Caribbean islands, where fruits abound. The bitterness
of the orange and the sweetness of the caramel melt
together with the pungent muskiness of the cloves.
Although the amount of cloves used in this recipe might
seem high, I am always surprised by the volume of spices
that can go into cakes. The sugar, almonds and polenta
just seem to absorb their flavour.

Preheat the oven to 180°C/350°F/gas 4. Butter a 20cm
(8in) round cake tin and line with baking paper. Lay the
orange slices over the base of the tin.

Place the chopped oranges in a pan of water and bring
to the boil. Cook for 20 minutes, then drain. Transfer to
a blender (or use a hand blender) and blend until almost
smooth.

In a bowl, cream the butter and 180g (6¼oz) of the
sugar until light and fluffy. Add the eggs, one at a time,
combining well between each addition. Mix in the blended
oranges, then fold in two-thirds of the ground cloves,
followed by the baking powder, flour, polenta and ground
almonds. Pour the mixture into the cake tin and bake for
1 hour, or until a skewer inserted into the middle of the
cake comes out clean. Allow the cake to cool in its tin
for 10 minutes, then turn out onto a plate.

To make the clove and orange caramel, heat the rest
of the sugar and the orange juice in a heavy-based pan,
until the sugar has dissolved and the liquid has thickened.
When it turns golden brown, immediately take it off the
heat and stir in the remaining ground cloves. Add a splash
of water if the caramel is too thick to drizzle – it should
be the consistency of honey. Drizzle the syrup all over the
cake and serve with a dollop of crème fraîche or yoghurt.

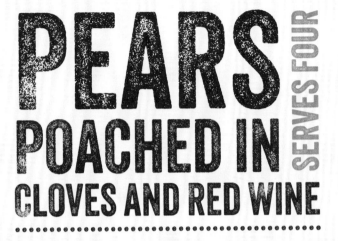

PEARS POACHED IN CLOVES AND RED WINE

SERVES FOUR

PREP: 10 MINS
COOK: 25–35 MINS

4 pears, peeled but left
    whole with stalks intact
4 tbsp honey
6 whole cloves
about 600ml (1 pint) red wine

To serve:
crème fraîche

This incredibly easy recipe tastes deliciously like the French classic, but with a warm clovey undertone. You can substitute apples or quince for the pears, if you like. Sometimes I splash a tiny bit of grappa on to the pears just before eating them for an extra kick.

Sit the pears in a suitably-sized pan so they fit snugly. Spoon in the honey, drop in the cloves and pour in enough red wine to cover them. Bring to the boil, then turn down to a simmer and poach for about 20–30 minutes, until softened but still firm.

Using a slotted spoon, remove the pears to serving plates. Bring the liquid back up to the boil and cook for 5 minutes, until it's reduced to a syrup. Pour the syrup over the pears and serve with crème fraîche.

CLOVES
SWEET
THINGS

SPICE ICE CREAM

SERVES SIX

PREP: 15 MINS
+ 30 MINS CHURNING

500ml (18fl oz) milk
500ml (18fl oz) double cream
3 green cardamom pods,
    seeds to be used and
    shells discarded
4 whole cloves
4 black peppercorns
4cm (1½in) cinnamon stick
1 English breakfast teabag
8 egg yolks
200g (7oz) sugar
½ tsp ground cloves mixed
    with a good pinch of freshly
    ground black pepper, to
    finish

This is a brilliant ice cream, which tastes a bit like the delicious chai tea that's drunk in India. You will need an ice cream maker for this.

In a large pan, heat the milk, cream, cardamom seeds, cloves, peppercorns and cinnamon together for 10 minutes until just about to boil. Take off the heat and add the teabag. Then set aside.

In a large bowl, whisk the egg yolks with the sugar, then slowly add the hot milk mixture, whisking constantly.

Return the egg and milk mixture to the pan and cook slowly, stirring with a wooden spoon until the mixture is thick enough to coat the back of a spoon. Leave to cool, then pass through a sieve to remove the whole spices. Transfer to an ice-cream maker and churn until frozen. Just before you serve the ice cream, swirl through the ground cloves and black pepper.

EMMA'S CLOVE THERAPIES

The clove is a powerhouse of a spice. It is the champion of all antioxidants – a drop of clove oil contains 400 more per unit volume than goji berries, the most powerful of all known antioxidant fruits.

For centuries cloves have been used in dentistry: they're a common ingredient in toothpastes, make a natural and effective mouthwash as the eugenol in them has a refreshing, menthol-like flavour, and they're a top-notch cure for toothache due to their numbing, analgesic properties. Cloves are also anti-inflammatory, antibacterial, antiviral, antifungal – pretty much 'anti' anything that is a potential threat to health!

In Zanzibar I was interested to learn that cloves are commonly used as a stomach calmer. Apparently it's due to the 'anthelmintics' that kill off nasty parasites in the stomach. Handy to know if, like me, you suffer from tummy troubles when travelling.

Cloves are a warming spice, which is probably why they're used extensively in Britain at Christmas time; but a lively trip to a Zanzibarian spa opened my eyes to their topical use as a refreshing and cooling scrub.

THE STORY OF CLOVES

Cloves are native to the Moluccas, or 'Spice Islands', in Indonesia and were one of the first spices to be traded – archaeologists have found evidence of cloves in Syrua dating as far back as 1721 BC. The Dutch dominated the spice trade in the 17th century and, in order to maintain their monopoly, they destroyed any trees outside their control.

Ferocious wars were fought and many people lost their lives trying to break the Dutch monopoly over this precious spice. In 1770 the Frenchman Peter Poivre (the same Peter Piper in the well-known tongue-twister) smuggled seedlings out of Indonesia, breaking the Dutch monopoly, and it was those seedlings that found their way to Zanzibar, now the world's leading producer of the spice.

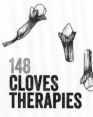

MEDICINAL USES

■ Clove honey is believed to be the most powerful medicine on the island of Zanzibar and in particular is thought to protect those suffering from bone conditions, as well as to prevent flu, colds and fever. It's also given to children to protect them from infection. (See recipe overleaf.)

■ Cloves are good for the digestive system – eating cloves increases hydrochloric acid in the stomach, thereby acting as a carminative.

■ The clove's antiseptic antibacterial properties can help relieve symptoms of bronchitis and asthma.

■ Ground cloves can be applied topically to help treat athlete's foot and other fungal infections.

■ According to folklore, sucking on 2 cloves without chewing or swallowing helps to curb the desire for alcohol.

■ Toasted cloves make a fantastically fragrant incense – their spicy aroma can help relieve fatigue, drowsiness and headaches.

■ An orange studded with cloves is commonly used as a pomander, filling the house with a delicious scent at Christmas.

A NOTE OF WARNING

The clove oil that is sold commercially is for external use only. Clove oil is only ever ingested when it is part of cough syrup or medicine.

ANTISEPTIC CLOVE HONEY

This is a natural antiseptic for treating bee stings and insect bites, rashes, cuts, bruises, acne, styes and sores. Caryophyllene, found in cloves, has strong anti-inflammatory properties and can reduce redness. I have even allowed myself to be bitten to test this theory, so I know it works!

To make clove honey, mix 1 teaspoon of ground cloves with 2 teaspoons of honey and a splash of water. To gain benefits, take one teaspoon a day.

CLOVE MOUTHWASH AND STOMACH CALMER

Chewing on a clove is an age-old remedy for toothache. This powerful breath freshener helps maintain healthy gums and heal ulcers. (You can also drink this to aid digestion and ease stomach upsets, vomiting and nausea as cloves help to relax the smooth muscle lining of the digestive tract.)

To make clove mouthwash simmer 300ml (½ pint) water with 1 tablespoon of cloves, leave to cool and then strain.

CLOVE AND ROSE BODY SCRUB

In Zanzibar young brides and grooms are traditionally cleansed with a scrub made from ground cloves, rose water and coconut oil to bring them protection.

The eugenol found in cloves makes this scrub fantastically cooling on the skin. It's refreshing, calming and totally natural. Your skin will be smooth and you'll smell wonderful!

It takes a bit of time to source the fantastic array of flowers used – available in some natural pharmacies or online – but it's worth the effort.

3 tbsp whole cloves, coarsely ground
2 tbsp rose water
2 tbsp coconut, almond or jojoba oil
3 tbsp coarsely ground dried flowers (a combination of dried rose petals, dried jasmine flowers, dried sandalwood, dried ylang ylang and dried sweet basil leaves)

Mix all the ingredients together to form a slightly loose, coarse and fragrant scrub.

To use, rub it vigorously into dry skin, then rinse off.

MULLED WINE

This recipe is so easy to make. For a virgin version with an uncannily similar flavour, use pomegranate juice instead of the red wine.

2 cinnamon sticks
2 mace blades
a pinch of whole cloves
3 star anise
3 tsp allspice
2 bottles of red wine
a few slices of orange
sugar, to taste

Put all the ingredients into a large saucepan and heat without letting it boil (this may make the spices bitter). Allow to simmer for at least half an hour, ladle into cups and serve.

'THE CLOVE IS A POWERHOUSE OF A SPICE. IT IS THE CHAMPION OF ALL ANTIOXIDANTS'

CUMIN
TURKEY
4

'LOCALS SAY THAT WHEN CUMIN IS USED IN COOKING, PEOPLE WANT TO JOIN IN THE EATING; FAMILY, FRIENDS AND PASSERS-BY DON'T STRAY FAR FROM THE TABLE WHEN THE FOOD IS THIS GOOD!'

Cumin is a wonderful spice. It might not have the glamour of cardamom or the sexiness of saffron but it's really special stuff. On first encounter it can seem a little dull, almost like the geeky bloke who lives next door, but as soon as you heat the seed it transforms, with flavours of orange groves, wet soil and sandalwood coiling up from the pan.

We travelled to Turkey to find out more about this commonly used, but rarely understood spice. Cumin is used all over the world and particularly revered in India and the Middle East, although it's pretty much only grown commercially in India and Turkey. It pops up in loads of spice blends as it brings depth and roundness to everything it's cooked with.

One of my favourite things to eat is a salad made with a spoonful of cumin seeds crackled in a pan with chillies, fresh tomatoes and a whole bunch of chopped coriander. It's a fast, simple dinner made interesting by the addition of exotic cumin. Cumin also goes really well with chickpeas, beef, lamb, tomatoes, beetroot, carrots and aubergines.

Cooking with cumin is pretty straightforward as long as you remember to heat the seeds to release their flavour. Once it's toasted and roughly ground, you can start adding cumin to salads and sprinkling it over roasted meat or vegetables. It rarely works well with fish although there are a few good exceptions, such as some fish curries and Moroccan tagines, but I'd always use it sparingly. Besides that, there are few rules. Just have a bowl of it toasted and roughly ground alongside your salt and pepper next time you cook and see what happens.

This humble little everyday spice is used generously in dishes around the world. Turkey is one of the world's largest cumin growers, and cumin is deeply embedded in all aspects of Turkish life. All that cumin symbolises is reflected in Turkish culture and the warm, welcoming nature of its people. There's a fantastic mist of magic and folklore surrounding cumin, enriching its personality and shrouding it in a mystery and power that takes it far away from the plain-looking seed sitting at the back of the cupboard.

It's said that cumin is a spice which binds and promotes love and family unity. In Turkey I discovered that this 'magic property' has far more to do with the unanimous love of food laced with cumin and much less to do with any kind of witchery: the locals say that when cumin's used in cooking, people want to join in the eating; family, friends and passers-by don't stray far from the table when the food is this good!

Cumin is best bought in whole-seed form and then freshly ground as and when required. Keep the seeds in an airtight glass jar and use within three months. When its pungent smell starts to diminish so will its flavour. I prefer to lightly toast the seeds before grinding them as this adds a savoury, nutty background depth to dishes and removes the overpowering soapy taste that is sometimes present and can be off-putting.

EGG, POTATO AND GREEN OLIVE PITTA

SERVES ONE

PREP & COOK: 7 MINS

1 x 100g (3½oz) floury potato
1 egg
about 5 green olives, stoned
   and roughly chopped
a small bunch of fresh
   coriander leaves
1 large pitta or flatbread
a pinch of cumin seeds,
   toasted then bashed
   with a pinch of sea salt
extra-virgin olive oil
table salt, for potato water

This sounds like an odd combination but it's classic Moroccan street food and tastes amazing. It's like eating a potato salad sandwich – not that different from a chip butty.

Boil the potato in salted water until soft, adding the egg to the pan for the last 5 minutes (ideally you want it soft-boiled, not runny). When the potato and egg are cool enough to handle, peel both, then roughly chop together and transfer to a bowl. Stir in the olives and tear in the coriander leaves.

Heat the pitta bread and split it open. Spoon in the egg mixture, sprinkle with the cumin salt and drizzle generously with olive oil. Fold up the sides of the bread and serve.

EMMA'S ONE-POT TOMATO AND FETA BAKED EGGS

SERVES FOUR

PREP: 10 MINS
COOK: 50 MINS

olive oil
3 peppers (green, red or a
    mixture of both), seeded and
    chopped into small chunks
1 onion, thinly sliced
4 garlic cloves, crushed
1 tsp sea salt
1 tsp sweet paprika
1 tsp cumin seeds, toasted
1 tsp dried chilli flakes
½ tsp toasted coriander seeds
½ tsp ground cumin
a pinch of freshly ground
    black pepper
2 x 400g tins chopped
    tomatoes
4 eggs
½ a block feta, crumbled

To serve:
pitta or other flatbreads

An exciting way to eat eggs, this is rich, tangy and full of fragrant spices that will really make your day go with a bang. It's so simple to prepare, in just one pot, that you're bound to have this on your table at least once a week – for breakfast, brunch or even dinner.

Heat a good glug of oil in a large, heavy-based frying pan (with a lid), and fry the peppers and onion over a medium heat until soft (about 10 minutes or more). Add the garlic and salt and continue to fry for 5 more minutes.

Add the spices, stir it all together and tip in the tinned tomatoes. Cover and cook for 40 minutes, then remove the lid and cook, uncovered, for a further 5 minutes.

Make 4 little wells in the mixture, break the eggs into these wells, re-cover and continue to cook for 5 minutes. Meanwhile, preheat the grill to high.

Uncover the pan and sprinkle a good handful of feta over the eggs. Place the pan under the grill for a few minutes to melt the cheese and ensure the eggs are cooked before serving with pitta or other flatbread.

CUMIN AND COURGETTE FRITTERS MAKES TWELVE

PREP & COOK: 10 MINS

250g (10oz) chickpea (gram) flour
2 tsp cumin seeds, toasted and ground
2 courgettes
2 red chillies, seeded and finely chopped
1 small bunch of coriander, roughly chopped
vegetable oil, for frying
sea salt

I think of this as a brilliant base recipe – you can replace the courgettes with anything from prawns to squash, potato or onion. These fritters are delicious served with a cold beer on a hot day. Chickpea flour (called gram flour in India) is a brilliant gluten-free flour used all over the world in all sorts of dishes.

Make a batter by carefully stirring about 400ml (¾ pint) cold water into the gram flour until it has the consistency of double cream. Mix the ground cumin seeds into the batter along with a good pinch of salt.

Using the coarse side of a grater, grate the courgettes into the batter, and add the chillies and coriander.

In a deep frying pan add vegetable oil to a depth of about 3cm (1¼in) and heat to about 180°C – you can test the temperature by dropping in a bit of bread; if turns golden in about 30 seconds, then the oil is at the right temperature.

Add small golf-ball-sized spoonfuls of the mixture, about 3 or 4 at a time, flatten a little with the back of a spoon and cook for 3 minutes on each side until the fritters are golden and crisp. Remove with a slotted spoon and leave to drain on a piece of kitchen paper while cooking the remaining fritters. Sprinkle with salt before serving nice and hot.

FRIED AUBERGINE
WITH TOMATO SAUCE AND CUMIN SALT

PREP: 10 MINS
COOK: 35 MINS

olive oil
1 garlic clove, finely sliced
1 x 400g tin plum tomatoes,
  drained and rinsed, or 5
  fresh plum tomatoes, peeled
1 tsp dried chilli flakes
2 tbsp sherry vinegar
2 aubergines, sliced in ½cm
  (¼in) discs
1 heaped tsp cumin seeds,
  toasted
sea salt and freshly ground
  black pepper

To serve:
feta (optional)

This is just as good served warm or at room temperature, either as part of a mezze or with a chunk of bread as a light lunch.

Add a good glug of oil to a pan and gently fry the garlic over a low heat until it starts to stick together. Pour in the tomatoes, breaking them up with the back of a wooden spoon. Season and add the chilli. Bring to the boil, then turn down and leave to simmer for about 30 minutes, until thick and sweet. Stir in the vinegar.

Meanwhile, heat a good drizzle of oil in a large, heavy-based frying pan. When the oil's nice and hot, sprinkle the aubergine slices with a little salt and fry on each side until soft and golden, about 5 minutes. Add more oil if necessary. When cooked, transfer to kitchen paper to drain. Keep warm if you want to serve the dish hot.

In a pestle and mortar, grind together the cumin with a pinch each of salt and pepper until fine.

Divide the aubergine between your serving plates, or lay it out on a platter and dollop the tomato sauce over it. Sprinkle with the cumin seasoning and feta if using.

CUMIN RULES

GENERAL RULES FOR COOKING WITH CUMIN

Whole cumin: Whole seeds are usually added to hot oil at the start of the cooking process to give a nutty flavour to the finished dish.

Ground cumin: When using shop-bought ground cumin, err on the side of generosity as it will have lost a lot of its flavour. Much better to dry-fry and grind your own.

Toasting cumin seeds: Keep the heat low and shake constantly. You'll know they're done when you're hit by the smell. The heat releases the fragrant essential oils, and this enhances the flavour of the spice. Always let the roasted spice cool before grinding them otherwise they won't break down properly.

STORAGE

Whole seeds: Will keep for about a year in a dry container out of direct sunlight.

Powder: As soon as the seeds are ground the flavourful oils start to evaporate, so if you've had a jar of cumin for a year or more throw it out. Ground cumin doesn't retain its quality for more than a few months.

BLACK CUMIN

There are two types of black cumin: Himalayan black cumin, which looks just like a black version or regular cumin; and the black cumin that is also commonly known as kalonji or nigella (*Nigella sativa*), which is incredibly high in vitamins C and E, boosts immunity and is said to 'cure all ills except death'.

This little black seed is renowned for its health-giving properties and is the secret ingredient in rural Turkish magic and myth. It contains essential amino acids, fatty acids, vitamins, calcium and potassium, and is the only plant found to contain the antioxidant Thymoquinone, which has been shown to increase by 30 per cent the natural cells the body uses to fight viruses.

In Turkey, black cumin smoke is thought to bind people together and the uncooked seeds are placed under children's pillows to keep them safe from harm.

Black cumin is widely used in Indian cooking, particularly in chutneys, pickles, korma sauces and garam masala mixes. It is also the seed sprinkled over peshawari naan and is used to flavour Middle Eastern breads.

BEETROOT AND TOMATO SALAD

WITH CUMIN AND HERB DRESSING

PREP & COOK: 25 MINS

about 15 golf-ball-sized
beetroots, red or golden,
scrubbed and trimmed
¼ garlic clove
a small handful each of fresh
marjoram and dill, plus
extra to garnish
1 heaped tsp cumin seeds,
toasted
a pinch of dried chilli flakes,
or ½ tsp chopped red chilli
juice of 1 lemon
olive oil
3–4 large tomatoes
a handful of celery leaves
½ celery heart, thinly sliced
sea salt and freshly ground
black pepper

Beetroot goes surprisingly well with cumin. I think the earthy notes in both ingredients get on well with each other.

In a large pan of boiling water (use separate pans for red and golden beetroots), cook the beetroots until tender and you can easily insert a knife into them (about 15–20 minutes, depending on the size of your beets). Remove from the boiling water, rinse under cold water to cool them down and then peel away the skin – it should come off easily if you rub the beets between your hands (you might want to wear gloves if you don't fancy having red hands all day).

On a large chopping board, finely chop the garlic and herbs together, adding the cumin seeds right at the end so they get lightly crushed. Transfer to a bowl, sprinkle in the chilli, squeeze in the lemon and add a good glug of oil so everything is submerged, and mix well.

Cut the tomatoes and beetroots to about ½cm (¼in) slices and divide between your serving plates, or lay out on a platter. Add the celery leaves and sliced celery. Season with salt and pepper, drizzle with the herb and cumin dressing and scatter with a few herbs to garnish.

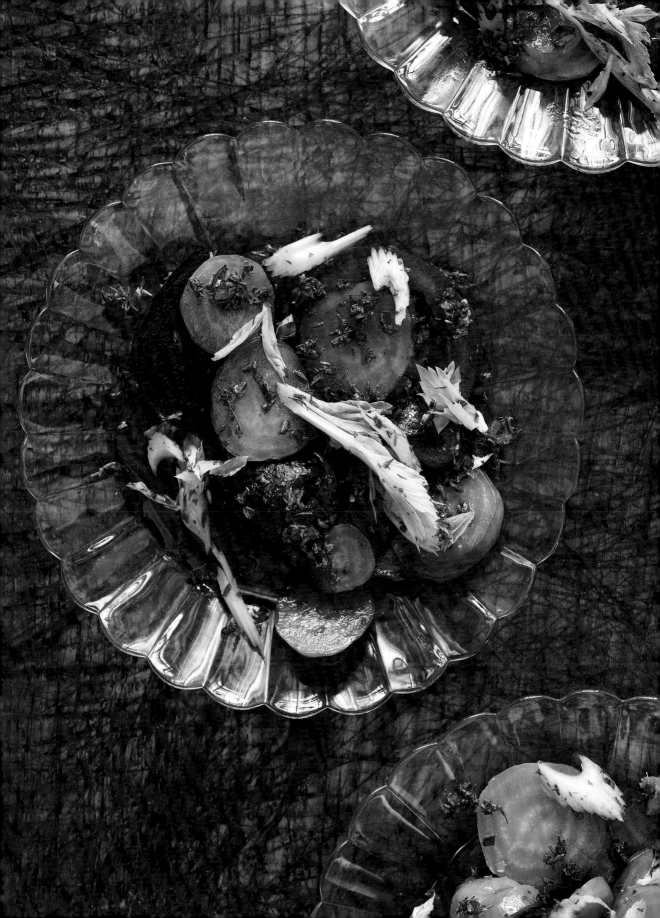

MOROCCAN CHILLI CUMIN SAUCE

MAKES 350G

PREP & COOK: 30 MINS

2 red peppers, chargrilled
  and peeled
4 tomatoes
olive oil
5 garlic cloves
20 mild red chillies, split in
  half and seeds removed
2 tsp cumin seeds, toasted
1 tsp caraway seeds
2 tsp sweet mild paprika
3 tbsp sherry vinegar
sea salt

This hot chilli sauce (*harissa*) is brilliantly useful. It's North African in origin, but if you have some in the fridge it'll find its way onto everything from pasta to a cheese sandwich. The cumin really underpins all the other flavours giving it an earthy, heady intensity.

Preheat the oven to 180°C/350°F/gas 4.

Roast the peppers with two of the tomatoes, a little olive oil and a good pinch of salt for 20 minutes, until soft.

Crush the garlic in a pestle and mortar with a little salt, then put into a blender with the chillies, the 2 raw tomatoes, the roasted pepper and roasted tomatoes and the spices. Pulse until you get a medium-fine texture, being careful not to overblend, it shouldn't be smooth. Stir in the sherry vinegar and enough olive oil to loosen the whole mixture and give the consistency of a thick, rich sauce.

CUMIN AND CORIANDER CHICKEN LIVERS

SERVES 4–6

PREP & COOK: 10 MINS

2 bunches of coriander
2 garlic cloves, peeled
1 x 5cm (2in) piece ginger
1 green chilli
a handful of cumin seeds, toasted and ground
juice of 1 lime, plus a squeeze for serving
olive oil
400g (14oz) chicken livers, trimmed
2 tbsp natural yoghurt
sea salt and freshly ground black pepper

To serve:
flatbread

This is quite a wet dish, so it's best to serve it in a bowl, preferably with flatbread. The sauce is a green masala (*hara masala*), which you can add to lots of things from clams to fish to roast chicken. It's like the Indian version of the *chermoula* on Emma's Zingy Roast Chicken (see page 178).

In a food processor, blend the coriander, ginger, chilli, spices and lime juice with a glug of oil until you have a wet green paste. Season to taste. Transfer to a bowl and toss with the chicken livers.

Heat a drizzle of oil in a large, heavy-based pan. When hot, add the livers and cook for 3–4 minutes, turning once. Take off the heat, stir in the yoghurt and serve in bowls. Add an extra squeeze of lime to taste. Serve with a pile of flatbread.

EMMA'S PARCEL OF CARROTS

WITH CUMIN, THYME AND WHITE WINE

SERVES FOUR

PREP: 10 MINS
COOK: 45 MINS

800g (1¾lb) carrots, thickly
   sliced, or small similar-sized
   Chantenay carrots
a small glass of white wine
a few thyme sprigs
a few knobs of butter or a glug
   of olive oil
a few garlic cloves, smashed
   in their skins
2 tsp cumin seeds, toasted
½ tsp sea salt

The beauty of cooking 'in a bag' or parcel is twofold; it's quick to prepare and mingles the flavours wonderfully by both steaming and baking at the same time. These carrots go with anything from pan-fried fish to a Sunday roast.

Preheat the oven to 220°C/425°F/gas 7.

Make a parcel using a double sheet of greaseproof paper or tinfoil. Put all the ingredients in the parcel and toss until the carrots are coated. Seal the parcel and place on a baking sheet.

Roast for 45 minutes, or until the carrots are soft, or reduce the cooking time a little if you prefer them slightly crunchy.

TURKISH PIZZA

MAKES FOUR

PREP & COOK: 15 MINS

For the dough:
350ml (12fl oz) lukewarm
    water (around 37°C)
1 tbsp dried yeast
a pinch of sugar
2 tbsp olive oil
500g (1¼lb) strong white
    bread flour (or 00 pasta
    flour), plus extra for dusting
½ tsp table salt

For the topping:
300g (11oz) lamb mince
1 red onion, chopped
1 tomato, chopped
1 green chilli, chopped
2 garlic cloves, chopped
2 tsp cumin seeds
1 tsp ground coriander
a pinch of Turkish chilli
    flakes, or 1 red chilli,
    finely chopped (optional)
1 tsp sumac (optional)
a squeeze of lemon juice
sea salt

To serve:
a large handful of parsley
    leaves
a large handful of mint leaves

These are called *Lahmacun* in Turkey and they're one of my favourite snacks. This is a classic version, but there are loads of different ones so experiment as you like. The dough keeps in the fridge overnight but needs an hour to wake up before you roll it.

In a bowl, mix the warm water with the yeast, sugar and oil. Leave for about 10 minutes to froth up. Meanwhile, mix the flour and salt in a large mixing bowl and make a well in the centre. Add the liquid, then stir, gradually incorporating all of the liquid to make a sticky dough.

Turn out the dough onto a well-floured surface and knead until it is transformed into a glossy, stretchy dough. Return to the bowl, cover tightly with clingfilm and leave somewhere warm for about 1 hour. Once risen, turn out again and knead for a few more minutes.

Preheat the oven to its hottest setting 230–300°C/450–475°F/gas 8–9 and put a pizza stone or heavy roasting tray in to get really hot.

On a large board, chop together the lamb, onion, tomato, green chilli, garlic, cumin and coriander to make a smooth mush. Season well.

On a well-floured surface, roll your dough into 4 large rounds, about ½cm (¼in) thick. Spread the lamb mix thinly on top of the dough. Remove the hot baking tray from the oven and very carefully transfer the *lahmacuns* onto it (you might find a tart tin base or something flat useful for this). Bake for about 5 minutes, until bubbly and slightly brown at the edges. Sprinkle with the chilli flakes and the sumac if you want. Add a squeeze of lemon and roll up with the parsley and mint leaves to eat.

TURKISH HUMMUS

SERVES FOUR

PREP & COOK: 5 MINS

1 garlic clove, peeled
2 x 400g tin chickpeas,
    drained and rinsed
1 heaped tbsp tahini
juice of 1 lemon
2 tsp cumin seeds,
    toasted and ground
extra-virgin olive oil
sea salt and freshly
    ground black pepper

To serve:
raw vegetables

A member of the parsley family (like dill and fennel), cumin grows wispy thin stems that flower into pretty, spindle-like flower wheels that develop into small seeds after a couple of weeks. The seeds are allowed to grow to a few millimetres, then picked while still green and threshed to remove a little of the husk and the stalks. It is a really easy spice to grow but, as we discovered in Turkey, incredibly hard work to harvest, not least because it's grown in arid, roasting-hot plains. Spending hours bent over in the sun was certainly too much for me – I had to run off and make this rich, heady, cumin-laced hummus. If you can get hold of them, jarred chickpeas are even better for this dish than tinned.

Using a pestle and mortar, pound the garlic and a good pinch of salt into a paste. If using a large pestle, add the chickpeas and continue bashing, or transfer to a food processor or blender. When you have a smoothish mixture (a bit of texture is nice), stir in the tahini, lemon juice and the ground cumin. Pour in about 200ml (7fl oz) oil, adding a little more if you feel it needs it. Season to taste and serve with raw vegetables.

REALLY EASY CUMIN LENTILS

**PREP & COOK:
1 HR 10 MINS**

200g (7oz) toor dhal lentils,
   rinsed
1 garlic clove, chopped
½ white onion, sliced
2 tomatoes, chopped
a pinch of sugar
a squeeze of lemon juice
4 tbsp olive oil
1 tbsp cumin seeds
3 whole dried mild chillies
a large handful of coriander
   leaves
sea salt and freshly ground
   black pepper

To serve:
chapattis

Dhal and chapatti is one of my 'desert island' choices
for things to eat. If you can't find toor lentils, substitute
channa dhal or yellow split peas.

In a large pan, cover the lentils, garlic, onion and
tomatoes with cold water and bring to the boil. Turn
down to a simmer and cook for about 1 hour, until the
lentils are soft. Season well, then stir in the sugar and
lemon juice, adding more to taste.

Heat the oil in a frying pan, and fry the cumin and
chillies until they begin to crackle. Stir into the dhal,
top with the coriander leaves and serve with chapattis.

CUMIN QUICK FIXES

■ Add powdered or whole seeds to pulses and tomatoey vegetable dishes, and leave to simmer for extra flavour.

■ Dry-fry whole cumin then bash with a pinch of salt, and sprinkle on a joint of roast lamb right at the end of cooking to retain the fragrance of toasted cumin. Lamb and cumin is a classic combo.

■ Cumin raita, made with toasted whole cumin, yoghurt, fresh mint and a squeeze of lemon is an authentic side dish and classic cooler for spicy curries. It also makes a good dip for flatbreads as part of a mezze.

■ Toasted cumin seeds are delicious sprinkled on avocado.

■ Black cumin (nigella or kalonji seeds): Toss potatoes or butternut squash in olive oil and black cumin seeds before roasting to give a nutty flavour to your roast.

CUMIN SPICE BLEND

2-parts toasted coarsely ground cumin seeds
1-part dried chilli flakes
1-part black pepper
salt, to taste

Uses: A dry dip for meat (especially lamb); a seasoning for yoghurt (add a crushed garlic clove and squeeze of lemon); a sprinkle seasoning for cooking meat.

EMMA'S ZINGY ROAST CHICKEN

**PREP: 25 MINS, PLUS
1–2 HRS MARINATING
COOK: 50–60 MINS**

8 chicken leg/thigh portions
    or 1 x 1.5kg (3¼lb) whole
    chicken
a good handful of coriander
a good handful of parsley
3–4 garlic cloves, peeled
zest of 1 lemon and juice of ½
1 small onion, sliced
olive oil
1 tsp salt

For the spice blend:
1 tbsp toasted ground cumin
1 tsp smoked or sweet paprika
    or cayenne pepper
½ tsp freshly ground black
    pepper

Good old roast chicken is an easy 'go to' dish and takes on the bright, earthy flavours of *chermoula* paste really well. The fresh paste combines cumin's savoury, nutty flavour with sweet paprika that contrasts with the zingy herbs. *Chermoula* is a North African paste normally used for marinating fish, but it also gives roast chicken an incredible flavour. Smother it on, let it infuse for as long as you can resist, and then roast to perfection. I cooked this dish for the workers on the cumin plantation in Turkey as a thank-you harvest supper, and they loved it.

In a blender or pestle and mortar (if using the latter you'll need to roughly chop the herbs, garlic and ½ the onion), combine the fresh coriander, parsley, garlic, lemon zest and juice, ½ the onion slices, a glug of olive oil, 1 tsp salt and the spices. Coarsely blend to make a thick paste.

Pull the skin away from the flesh of the chicken and press your fingers underneath. Levering the skin away from the meat, spoon the paste between the skin and flesh and massage over the top of each piece to spread the paste all over the flesh in every crease and crevice. Rub the rest of the paste over the outside of the chicken pieces. Leave to marinate for at least 1 hour.

When you're ready to roast the chicken, preheat the oven to 190°C/375°F/gas 5.

Arrange the remaining onion slices on the base of a roasting tray and sit the chicken on top. Roast for 30 minutes, then turn up the heat to 220°C/425°F/gas 7 and continue to roast for a further 20–30 minutes, until the juices run clear when a skewer is inserted into the flesh; if the chicken browns too quickly, loosely cover it with foil.

Remove from the oven, cover and set aside to rest for 10–15 minutes before serving.

CAULIFLOWER AND POTATO CURRY

PREP: 10 MINS
COOK: 25 MINS

4 large potatoes, peeled and
  cut into 2cm (¾in) cubes
olive oil, for frying
1 red onion, sliced
2 tbsp cumin seeds
1 x 5cm (2in) piece ginger,
  peeled and finely chopped
1 tbsp ground coriander
¼ tsp turmeric
½ tsp chilli powder
1 cauliflower, broken into
  large florets and leaves
  roughly chopped
a small bunch of coriander,
  leaves picked
3 tbsp Greek-style yoghurt
sea salt and freshly ground
  black pepper

This is a brilliant dish to know as it's incredibly cheap
and immensely satisfying. It's one I like to teach to people
going off to uni as it's a great healthy staple. It also makes
a terrific side dish for grilled meat or fish.

Bring the potatoes to the boil in a pan of salted water,
and cook until tender. Drain and leave to cool.

Heat a little oil in a large, heavy-based pan (with a lid),
and gently fry the onion until soft, about 5 minutes. Turn
up the heat and add the cumin seeds. When they begin
to crackle, add the ginger, ground coriander, turmeric
and chilli. Stir for 1 minute, adding a little extra oil if
it begins to stick.

Add the cauliflower, followed by 100ml (3½fl oz) water
and a good pinch of salt. Place the lid on the pan and
bring to the boil. Cook for 10 minutes, until the cauliflower
is just done. Stir in the potatoes and coriander and finish
by swirling in the yoghurt. Taste for seasoning, and serve.

STEAK WITH GRILLED VEGETABLES AND CUMIN AND GARLIC YOGHURT

SERVES FOUR

PREP & COOK: 30 MINS

4 x 200g (7oz) sirloin steaks
2 tsp dried oregano
olive oil
4 Turkish green peppers or
2 normal green peppers
1 aubergine, cut into 1cm
(½in) slices
4 courgettes, cut into ½cm
(¼in) slices
6 cherry tomatoes, halved
red wine vinegar
sea salt and freshly ground
black pepper
3 tbsp Emma's Cumin Spice
Blend (see page 174)

For the yoghurt dressing:
¼ garlic clove
1 heaped tsp cumin seeds,
toasted
6 tbsp Greek-style yoghurt,
plus extra for serving

I'm always looking for lighter ways to eat beef. People love to serve it with a substantial side and sauce, but sometimes it's just not what you feel like eating. Steak takes beautifully to grilled vegetables and yoghurt.

Place the steak in a bowl and toss with the dried oregano and a good glug of olive oil. Cover with clingfilm and leave to marinate at room temperature for 20 minutes.

Meanwhile, heat a griddle pan or barbecue until searingly hot. Grill the peppers until the skin is charred and the flesh soft, then transfer to a bowl, cover with clingfilm and leave to sweat.

Sprinkle the aubergine and courgette slices with salt, then grill on both sides until char marks appear and the vegetables are cooked through. Transfer to a bowl (but keep the griddle pan or barbecue hot).

Peel the peppers and discard the skin and seeds. Combine with the rest of the vegetables and the tomatoes. Add a splash of the vinegar, toss, then add a drizzle of oil and season.

To make the yoghurt dressing, in a pestle and mortar, bash the garlic into a paste with a pinch of salt. Add the cumin seeds, bash a couple of times to slightly crush them, then stir in the yoghurt and a little water. Stir until you have the consistency of double cream.

Season the steak and grill for 2–3 minutes on each side for medium rare. Transfer to a plate to rest for a few minutes. Serve with the grilled vegetables, a good drizzle of yoghurt and Emma's Cumin Spice Blend for extra pep.

MUSA'S CUMIN KÖFTE
WITH MELON AND TOMATO SALAD

PREP & COOK: 15 MINS

For the köfte:
1 small red onion, finely
    chopped
1 garlic clove, finely chopped
a handful of parsley leaves,
    finely chopped
a pinch of ground cinnamon
a pinch of ground allspice
a pinch of chilli flakes
1 tbsp ground cumin
250g (9oz) lamb mince
250g (9oz) beef mince
olive oil, for frying
sea salt and freshly
    ground black pepper

For the salad:
1kg (2¼lb) watermelon or
    other small melon, such
    as cantaloupe or galia,
    cut into large chunks
2 tomatoes, cut into large
    chunks
100g (3½oz) feta
a handful of mint leaves
1 chilli, finely chopped
olive oil
juice of 1 lemon
sea salt and freshly ground
    black pepper

Köfte are Turkish meatballs. Musa Dagdeviren at the Çiya restaurant in Istanbul taught me how to make his *köfte*. He always cuts the meat by hand (I used the biggest knife I've ever seen, though he wasn't too impressed with my knife skills). Of course, you can use minced meat, as I've done here – you won't quite get the crumbly texture of Musa's *köfte* but they'll still taste great. It's important to get enough fat in the mixture – as when making sausages or burgers – to keep the patties moist and tasty. I always use the beef fat as it's not as greasy as lamb fat. I like to serve these with a melon, tomato, chilli and feta salad.

Place all the *köfte* ingredients, except for the oil, in a large bowl and season well with salt and pepper. Mix everything with your hands until the mixture is just combined, but try not to overmix. With slightly wet hands, shape the meat into patties about 4cm (1½in) in diameter and press a finger in the middle of each patty to make an indentation.

To make the salad place the melon and tomatoes in a bowl and season. Break in the feta, tear in the mint, and sprinkle in the chilli. Drizzle generously with oil and squeeze the lemon juice over the salad. Toss very gently for a few seconds and then leave to sit while you cook the *köfte*.

Heat up a large pan with a good glug of oil. When the oil is hot, fry the *köfte* for 2 minutes on each side until golden and just cooked through. Serve with the salad.

CUMIN AND ORANGE MADEIRA CAKE

SERVES 12–16

PREP: 10 MINS
COOK: 45–60 MINS

125g (4½oz) butter, softened
125g (4½oz) sugar
3 eggs
1 tsp cumin seeds
zest of 1 orange
170g (5¾oz) self-raising
   flour, sifted
50g (2oz) ground almonds
2 tbsp milk

This is a variation on the classic seed cake. The traditional recipe uses caraway seeds but this version is perhaps even better with the earthy, citrus, exotic flavour of cumin, and it's really simple to make. It's the perfect afternoon cake.

Preheat the oven to 170°C/325°F/gas 3. Line a 20 x 9cm (8 x 3½in) loaf tin with baking paper.

In a large bowl, cream together the butter and sugar until light and fluffy. Beat in the eggs, one at a time, followed by the cumin, zest, flour, almonds and milk. Carefully pour into the loaf tin and bake in the oven for 45–60 minutes, until a skewer inserted into the centre of the cake comes out clean. Turn out on to a wire rack to cool.

PISTACHIO ROSE CAKE SERVES TWELVE

●●●●●●●●●●●●●●●●●●●●●●●●●●●●●●●●●●●●●●

PREP: 20 MINS
COOK: 20 MINS

12 filo pastry sheets, cut into
    30cm (12in) discs (use the
    base of a cake tin as a guide)
75g (2½oz) butter, melted
300g (11oz) pistachios,
    roughly chopped
1½ tbsp black cumin (nigella
    or kalonji) seeds
6 tbsp honey
6 tbsp rose water
500ml (18fl oz) double cream
dried or fresh rose petals,
    to decorate

This is almost a cake version of baklava. It's quite fun to make and really impressive to look at, although once you cut it it disintegrates into a mess. A delicious mess though. Try to find the tiny bright green, unripe pistachios. They're really amazing but do cost a pretty penny.

Preheat the oven to 160°C/325°F/gas 3. Line 2 baking trays with baking paper, then butter the baking paper.

On the baking tray, divide the filo discs into 3 piles, painting a little butter in between the layers of each pile. Mix the nuts with the cumin seeds, honey and 4 tablespoons of the rose water, then spread one-third of the mixture over each pile. You'll have 3 stacks of filo and pistachio mix. Bake in the oven for 20 minutes, until the pastry is golden. Leave to cool on the tray.

When cool, beat the cream with the remaining rose water until you have soft, undulating waves. Spread the cream over 2 of the pastry stacks, then layer the stacks on top of each other, finishing with the stack without cream. Scatter with the rose petals, and serve.

CUMIN LASSI

MAKES 2 GLASSES

PREP: 2 MINS

250g (9oz) yoghurt
pinch of cumin seeds, toasted
and lightly crushed
250ml (8fl oz) ice cold water
ice cubes
sea salt

This drink sounds a bit weird but it's amazingly good, especially on a hot day – you can pretend you're in Rajasthan in the sweltering, dusty heat with the incredible sounds and smells of Jaipur all around you.

Place the yoghurt and cumin seeds in a blender or cocktail shaker with the water and plenty of ice. Blend or shake well and pour into glasses. Stir in salt, to taste.

CUMIN BISCOTTI

MAKES TWENTY-FOUR

PREP: 10 MINS
COOK: 20–25 MINS

60g (2½oz) butter
115g (4oz) sugar
1 egg
125g (4¾oz) hazelnuts, roasted, then one-third finely chopped and two-thirds coarsely chopped
2 tsp black cumin (nigella or kalonji) seeds
160g (5½oz) plain flour, plus extra for dusting
2 tbsp semolina
1 tsp baking powder
½ tsp table salt

Preheat the oven to 160°C/325°F/gas 3. Line a baking tray with baking paper.

In a bowl, cream the butter with the sugar until light and fluffy. Beat in the egg.

In a separate bowl, combine the nuts, black cumin, flour, semolina, baking powder and salt. Mix until well combined. Stir the dry mixture into the creamed mixture to make a dough.

Divide the dough in half. On a very lightly floured surface, roll each half into logs, about 2½cm (1in) in diameter. Place, well spaced out, on the baking tray and bake for 15–20 minutes until golden and firm on the surface, but slightly yielding to the touch.

Transfer to a board and very carefully (you'll need a very sharp knife) slice the logs on an angle about 1cm (½in) thick. Place, cut-side down, on the warm baking tray and bake for another 5 minutes until golden. Transfer to a wire rack to cool.

EMMA'S CUMIN THERAPIES

Many spices are rich in vitamins and minerals — sometimes more so than the fresh fruit and veg that we know are good for us. Cumin is no exception.

Cumin has many therapeutic properties and has been used in folk and Ayurvedic medicines for hundreds of years. Unusually, it's thought to be both a warming and a cooling spice, with the ability to increase body heat and thereby speed up metabolism, which in turn boosts the immune system; while paradoxically it can also help keep the body cool, when drunk as cumin soda (see page 198) or in the yoghurt drink, lassi (see page 191). Totally amazing!

It's known that cumin can aid digestion — being a great source of dietary fibre — which is particularly useful in helping to maintain a healthy bowel. It's also thought to be an excellent tonic, supporting the digestive process and aiding elimination.

THE STORY OF CUMIN

Cumin has a 5000-year history — Egyptians used it in food and as part of the mummification process, while the Greeks and Romans used it in food and medicine. It's mentioned in the Bible that cumin was so highly prized for its medicinal benefits, it was used as currency to pay debts. In ancient Greece, carrying a large bag of cumin seeds was like carrying a wad of cash.

In ancient times, cumin seeds were a symbol of commitment, and married soldiers leaving for war were given wine infused with cumin or fresh cumin bread, baked by their wives, to prevent them straying.

A NOTE OF WARNING

While cumin is harmless for most people, a sensitivity to carrots, celery or coriander may increase the likelihood of an allergic reaction. Although in some cultures it's taken by nursing mothers to increase milk flow, pregnant or breastfeeding mothers are advised not to use cumin due to the lack of scientific research into its effects.

MEDICINAL USES

■ Like chilli, cumin is rich in vitamins A, B and C, which are potent antioxidants.

■ Cumin has as much as 1.3mg iron per teaspoon, so adding it to meals boosts your iron intake. It's especially good, therefore, for those suffering from anaemia.

■ Cumin has antiseptic qualities and is thought to help fight the common cold and flu by supporting the body's fight against infection.

■ Chewing on cumin and fennel seeds can help aid digestion after a meal.

■ Cumin is effective in reducing blood sugar; it aids production of the enzyme 'amylase', which breaks down sugars in the pancreas, the organ in which insulin is produced to regulate blood sugar. Diabetics should add cumin to their diet for this reason.

■ Cumin is a carminative (i.e. it relieves flatulence) and antispasmodic, and pairs beautifully with pulses such as chickpeas, helping to avoid the occasional embarrassing side effects that can come with them, along with any uncomfortable stomach cramps.

■ In folk medicine, fried cumin combined with ripe banana is recommended as a cure for insomnia.

■ Black cumin oil is great for the skin, being rich in vitamins C and E, which are essential for healthy, young-looking skin.

A TRIPLE CURE – CUMIN TEA

This infusion can be drunk to combat nausea, aid digestion and calm a crampy stomach. It can also be used as a remedy for skin conditions such as eczema, boils and dry skin. This method can also help fade burn marks and wrinkles.

Heat 1 litre (1¾ pints) of water in a pan to a gentle simmer. Add 1 tablespoon cumin seeds and simmer for 5–10 minutes. Strain and cool.

To apply, simply soak a bandage in the cool tea and apply to the affected area.

LIMEADE WITH A TWIST – REFRESHING CUMIN SODA

Cumin soda, or *jal jeera* as it's called in India, is commonly drunk in hot countries to keep the body cool. The cumin in this recipe stimulates the digestive system, while the mint triggers the body's cooling mechanisms, the salt rehydrates and the sugar provides energy. It's super-quick to make, refreshing and has a distinctive flavour. Serve, with or without sugar, as an aperitif to wake up the taste buds before a meal, or sweeten it and enjoy as a refreshing drink on its own. If you don't fancy mint leaves floating in your glass, blend the ingredients until smooth.

a handful of mint leaves
2 litres (3½ pints) soda water
1 tsp toasted ground cumin
½ tsp ground black pepper
juice of 2 limes
a good pinch of sea salt
1 heaped tbsp sugar

Bash the mint leaves between your palms to release their flavourful aroma, then place in a jug with the soda water, cumin and black pepper.

In a dish or pestle and mortar, mix together the lime juice, salt and sugar until the sugar has dissolved.

Add the sugar mixture to the soda water, stir until well combined (or use a blender, if preferred) and serve, with or without ice, in long glasses on hot days.

'CUMIN HAS MANY THERAPEUTIC PROPERTIES AND HAS BEEN USED IN FOLK AND AYURVEDIC MEDICINES FOR HUNDREDS OF YEARS. UNUSUALLY, IT'S THOUGHT TO BE BOTH A WARMING AND A COOLING SPICE, WITH THE ABILITY TO INCREASE BODY HEAT AND THEREBY SPEED UP METABOLISM, WHICH IN TURN BOOSTS THE IMMUNE SYSTEM; WHILE PARADOXICALLY IT CAN ALSO HELP KEEP THE BODY COOL, WHEN DRUNK AS CUMIN SODA OR IN THE YOGHURT DRINK, LASSI'

CINNAMON
INDIA
5

STEVIE

EMMA

Cinnamon is actually the bark of a tree, rather than a fruit or a seed like most spices. And it tastes like it, too, or at least the way you wish tree tasted. It has a wonderful deep, earthy, sweet smell that reminds me as much of coconut broth and travels in the East as it does Christmas at home with mulled wine and brandy. Delicate, yet so specific and unusual in flavour, cinnamon can stand up to all sorts of stronger tastes.

Cinnamon brings a wonderful, mouth-filling roundness to spice blends and something similar, but almost deeper, when thrown whole into slow-cooked stews or curries. Ground cinnamon gives a more immediate, more assertive flavour and is a useful baking ingredient.

In large quantities, however, cinnamon can be really cloying – think sticky American breakfast pastries. I wonder if this is because ground cinnamon is usually mostly made up of cassia. Cassia (*Cinnamomum cassia*) is a close relative of proper, or Ceylon cinnamon (*Cinnamomum verum*), and rather like delicate little cinnamon's brutish older brother – the one who got the brawn but not the looks. Cassia isn't always clearly labelled, so, to avoid overpowering your cooking, always buy whole cinnamon sticks that are soft enough to break in your hands, as these are likely to be true cinnamon and not its brutish older brother, cassia.

Cinnamon may be redolent of Christmas in the UK – but that's no reason to ignore it for the rest of the year. In Kerala it is used all year round, in curries, sambals, in rice and with meat.

I found Kerala both peaceful and vibrant. The colours and flavours are intense (as is the speed of the driving!) and yet there is a deep-rooted harmony and calm. We were lucky enough to sit in on a Hindu *pooja*, a Hindu ritual, led by a Brahman priest who was the most mesmerising person I've ever laid eyes on. The god Krishna was offered a cinnamon rice pudding, which we were told was his favourite. The whole experience was incredibly moving, with kids running in and out and a beautiful sense of acceptance.

Cinnamon has long been prized, and not only for its role in cooking: it was used in the embalming process in Ancient Egypt; offered as a gift for the god Apollo in Ancient Greece; and burnt on funeral pyres for wealthy Romans. Its source was kept secret by middlemen to protect their monopoly well into the 13th century: they told tall tales of giant birds that built nests high up in the trees; the gatherers lured them with heavy pieces of meat that knocked cinnamon sticks down from the trees as the birds flew back to their nests. These elaborate stories ensured that prices were kept sky high.

Thankfully, today it's far simpler for us to get hold of this wonderful spice. Buy good-quality cinnamon in stick form and it will keep well for quite long periods, or buy smaller quantities of ready-ground and replace regularly.

SWISS CHARD WITH CINNAMON
PINE NUTS, RAISINS AND VINEGAR

PREP & COOK: 25 MINS

1kg (2¼lb) Swiss or rainbow
    chard, leaves stripped from
    stalk, and stalk cut into
    1cm (¼in) strips
25g (1oz) butter
olive oil, for frying
1 shallot, finely sliced
2 garlic cloves, finely sliced
50g (2oz) pine nuts
6cm (2½in) cinnamon stick
a pinch of saffron threads,
    soaked in 2 tbsp boiling
    water
50g raisins, soaked in 2 tbsp
    red wine vinegar
sea salt and freshly ground
    black pepper

This is a great side dish, particularly with simply roasted chicken. Don't worry if you can only find Swiss chard with fine stalks or no stalks at all, as it's just as good. You can also use spinach instead of chard.

Bring a large pan of salted water to the boil. Blanch the chard leaves until soft, about 1 minute, then remove from the pan with a slotted spoon and lay them out on kitchen paper to drain and cool. In the same pan, boil the stalks until soft, about 10 minutes, then drain.

In a heavy-based pan, melt the butter with a splash of olive oil and gently fry the shallot with a pinch of salt over a low heat until soft and sweet, about 10 minutes. Add the garlic, pine nuts and the cinnamon stick and continue to fry, stirring occasionally, for 5 minutes, adding the saffron water and raisins for the final minute.

Roughly chop the chard leaves and add to the pan, along with the stalks. Give it a good mix, season well and serve.

SPICED FRIED POTATOES

PREP & COOK: 25 MINS

1kg (2¼lb) floury potatoes
such as King Edward
or Maris Piper, peeled
and cut into 2–3cm
(¾–1¼in) chunks
vegetable oil, for frying
table salt

For the spice mix:
1 tbsp green cardamom pods,
seeds removed and shells
discarded
1 tsp fennel seeds
1½ tsp coriander seeds,
toasted
½tsp whole cloves
4cm (1½in) cinnamon stick
1 tsp mustard seeds
¼ tsp turmeric
a pinch of chilli powder
sea salt

To serve:
yoghurt

You may have a little spice mix left over, but it's delicious sprinkled on anything from sliced tomatoes to boiled eggs. The yoghurt provides a refreshing and cool contrast to the hot, spicy potatoes. Great as a snack or side.

Grind the spices together in a spice grinder, or bash them in a pestle and mortar, until you have a fine powder. Pass through a sieve to remove any large bits if necessary.

Put the potatoes in a pan of salted water and bring to the boil. Reduce the heat to a simmer and cook for 8–10 minutes, or until tender. Drain in a colander, then place the colander over the hot pan to allow the potatoes to steam-dry.

Half-fill a large, heavy-based pan with oil and place over a medium heat. Test the heat of the oil with a chunk of bread; when the bread sizzles and gently turns golden in 30 seconds, the oil's hot enough. Carefully lower the potatoes into the oil and fry for 3–4 minutes, or until golden brown and crisp. Remove with a slotted spoon and drain on kitchen paper. Season the potatoes with salt and scatter generously with the spice mix. Serve with a good dollop of yoghurt on the side to dip the potatoes into.

CRISP CINNAMON LENTIL CAKES

MAKES FIFTEEN

PREP: 15 MINS
COOK: 20 MINS

125g (4¾oz) black mung beans
(or red lentils), soaked for
at least 6 hours (ideally
overnight)
½ tsp table salt
60g (2½oz) freshly grated
coconut
1 onion, finely chopped
1 garlic clove, crushed
with a pinch of salt
2cm (¾in) piece ginger,
peeled and grated
1 small green chilli,
finely chopped
20 fresh curry leaves,
roughly chopped
½ tsp turmeric
½ tsp chilli powder
1 tsp ground cinnamon
2 tsp cumin seeds
approx. 150g (5oz) fine
rice flour
vegetable oil, for frying
sea salt, to sprinkle

On trains in Sri Lanka you hear men marching the corridors chanting 'Wadiwadiwadiwadi'. They are advertising these wonderful snacks. They're perfect accompanied by a cold beer. Push a prawn into each cake before frying for a delicious treat. You'll need to start preparing these the night before you want to eat them.

Drain the beans or lentils and place in a bowl with the salt and everything but the flour and the oil. Stir well with a wooden spoon. Gradually add the flour, a handful at a time, followed by a splash of water, and mix. Keep adding the flour and water until the mixture comes together and holds its shape when you press a handful of it together.

With wet hands, take a tablespoonful of the mixture at a time, shape it into a ball and then flatten into a disc about 2cm (¾in) thick. Place the discs on a dampened plate while you heat the oil.

Half-fill a heavy-based pan with oil and put over a medium heat. Test the heat of the oil with a chunk of bread; when the bread sizzles and gently turns golden in 30 seconds, the oil's hot enough. Very carefully drop the lentil cakes into the oil and fry for 4–6 minutes until golden and cooked. (You may have to do this in batches.) Remove with a slotted spoon and drain on kitchen paper before serving piping hot sprinkled with sea salt.

CLAMS WITH TOMATO CURRY LEAVES AND CINNAMON

PREP & COOK: 5 MINS

1kg (2¾lb) clams, (preferably Palourde) rinsed
olive oil
a handful of curry leaves
1 small dried chilli or ½ tsp dried chilli flakes
8cm (3¼in) cinnamon stick, broken into pieces
2 tomatoes, peeled, seeds discarded and flesh chopped
2 tsp grated ginger

To serve:
toasted bread

Palourde clams (also known as carpet shell clams) are wonderful because they really taste of the sea. If you can't find them, use any other clam variety, or mussels would work well too. This is a perfect starter or light lunch.

Check that any partially open clams are alive by sliding a sharp knife in between the 2 halves of the shell. You want to feel the clam tense up; if the knife slips in easily, discard the clam. Closed clams are fine to use.

Heat a good glug of oil in a deep, heavy-based pan (with a lid), and fry the curry leaves, chilli and cinnamon for 1 minute over a medium heat. Add the clams followed by the tomatoes and ginger. Stir carefully with a spoon and put the lid on the pan and cook for about 2–3 minutes, or until all the clams are open. Serve in bowls with thick pieces of toasted bread.

SQUASH CINNAMON HAZELNUT AND QUINOA SALAD

SERVES EIGHT

PREP: 10 MINS
COOK: 45 MINS

1.5kg (3¼lb) butternut
squash, peeled, seeds
discarded and flesh cut
into 4cm (1½in) chunks
1 red chilli, seeded and sliced
10cm (4in) cinnamon stick,
broken into 3
¼ bunch oregano or marjoram,
leaves picked
olive oil,
150g (5oz) quinoa, rinsed
juice of ½ lemon
a small bunch of watercress,
roughly chopped
150g (5oz) hazelnuts, roasted
and roughly crushed
sea salt and freshly ground
black pepper

For years I was put off eating quinoa because of the snobbery surrounding its name (it's keenoiaah, darling) and the fact that it seems like a bit of a hippy ingredient. I now realise I've been missing out. It is wonderful stuff.

Preheat the oven to 200°C/400°F/gas 6.

Place the squash in a large bowl along with the red chilli, cinnamon and oregano. Season generously, drizzle with oil and toss until everything is well coated. Transfer to a baking tray, cover with tinfoil and bake for 45 minutes, removing the foil for the last 15 minutes. Remove from the oven and keep warm. The squash should be golden and soft. If not, return it to the oven.

Meanwhile, cook the quinoa according to packet instructions, then drain and leave to steam-dry. Season to taste, drizzle with oil and squeeze the lemon juice over it. Stir lightly and leave to cool.

Add the watercress to the cooled quinoa and toss well to coat. Divide half the mixture between your plates, top with the squash, then scatter the remaining quinoa over the top and sprinkle with the roasted hazelnuts.

EMMA'S TOMATO
CURRY SERVES FOUR

PREP TIME: 5 MINS
COOK TIME: 15 MINS

2 tbsp olive oil
1 red onion, finely diced
3 garlic cloves, finely diced
3cm (1¼in) piece ginger,
   peeled and chopped
1 cinnamon stick
a generous pinch of curry
   leaves
½ tsp green cardamom pods
1 tsp ground cinnamon
1 tsp ground coriander
1 tsp ground cumin
a pinch of ground cloves
½ tsp chilli powder
¼ tsp turmeric
¾ tsp dried fenugreek leaves
500g (1lb 2oz) cherry
   tomatoes, halved
½ tsp sea salt

To serve:
chapattis (optional)

A quick and fresh cherry tomato curry, similar to the Indian *Thakkali Kulambu*, that celebrates the natural flavour of really good tomatoes.

Heat the oil in a heavy-based pan and fry the diced onion for a few minutes, then add the garlic, ginger, cinnamon, curry leaves and cardamom and fry until the onion is soft and garlic is golden.

Add the remaining spices, stir for a minute, then add half the tomatoes, the ½ teaspoon of salt and 100ml (3½fl oz) water, and simmer until the tomatoes have broken down into a thick sauce.

Add the remaining tomatoes, simmer for a further 5 minutes and then turn off the heat so they don't break down too much. This is lovely served with chapattis.

CINNAMON QUICK FIXES

- Cinnamon toast – eggy bread with loads of cinnamon! A hit with kids

- Warm a pan of cloudy apple juice with cinnamon and cloves for a spicy winter warmer

- For a warming winter custard add a teaspoon of ground cinnamon

- A stick of cinnamon in a stew brings out the deep meaty flavours of lamb, beef and chicken and adds warmth and depth in the winter

- Cinnamon tea – a broken cinnamon quill steeped in hot water is great for health and very warming in winter

CINNAMON GARAM MASALA

2 tbsp ground cinnamon
2 tbsp ground fennel
1 tsp ground cardamon
1 tsp ground black pepper
1 tsp ground nutmeg
½ tsp ground cloves

Uses: Add to curries during cooking for extra aroma and complexity; add to mashed potato to make 'masala mash'; rub onto roast meats or root vegetables; toast and sprinkle over Indian food such as curries, chutneys and salads.

CINNAMON RULES

It's hard to grind your own cinnamon sticks to a fine powder, so best to keep both sticks and powder in the cupboard. If you're cooking an American recipe, increase the amount of cinnamon to compensate for the stronger cassia cinnamon they use in the States.

STORAGE

Whole: Sticks will last about a year stored in an airtight container.

Ground: In an airtight container out of direct sunlight, ground cinnamon will last about 6 months.

219
**CINNAMON
QUICK
FIXES**

CINNAMON RICE AND PEAS WITH YOGHURT AND SWEET HERBS

PREP: 20 MINS
COOK: 15 MINS

50g (2oz) butter
2 red onions, sliced
sea salt
3 big handfuls of fresh
    or frozen peas
300g (11oz) basmati rice,
    soaked in water for at
    least 1 hour

For the spice mix:
½ tsp coriander seeds
½ tsp cumin seeds
½ tsp ground allspice
3 whole cloves
10 black peppercorns
¼ nutmeg
6cm (2½in) cinnamon stick

To serve:
1 tbsp Greek-style yoghurt
2 big handfuls of chopped
    herbs, ideally a mixture
    of parsley, dill and mint
sumac (optional)
dried chilli flakes (optional)

I'm always making pilafs, varying them with the seasons and what I have around — anything from cauliflower to pistachio — adjusting the spices accordingly. A fluffy pilaf is a thing of beauty, just make sure you wash the rice well and follow the instructions for water and timings and you'll find you have rice fit for a king.

Prepare the spice mix by placing all the whole spices, except for the nutmeg and cinnamon, in a food processor or spice grinder, and grinding everything to a fine powder (or bashing the spices in a pestle and mortar). Stir in the grated nutmeg. Put to one side.

Heat the butter in a deep, heavy-based pan (one with a tight-fitting lid). Cook the onions gently in the butter with a good pinch of salt until soft but not mushy. Add the peas, spice mix and the cinnamon stick. Continue cooking for about 5 minutes. Drain the soaked rice, taking care not to break up the grains.

Turn up the heat so the onions are sizzling and add the rice and a good pinch of sea salt. Carefully stir the onions through the rice, to mix in. Add sufficient hot water to come 2.5cm (1in) above the rice. The water must be just off the boil and the base of the pan should be hot. Stir once to mix. When the water begins to simmer, cut a circle out of greaseproof paper large enough to cover the pan. Place the lid on top of the paper so it fits tightly. Turn the heat up high, cook for 4 minutes, then reduce the heat to low and cook for a further 6 minutes.

Take the pan off the heat and leave the pilaf to rest, covered, for about 10 minutes — resist the temptation to take off the lid. Once it has rested, fluff the pilaf up slightly with a fork, then mix in the yoghurt and a handful of herbs. To serve, sprinkle with the remainder of the chopped herbs, and some sumac and dried chilli flakes if you have them.

BOAT TIMINGS

6.40	1.40
7.05	2.30
7.45	3.00
8.15	3.30
8.40	4.00
9.05	4.40
9.35	5.05
10.10	5.35
10.35	6.00
11.10	7.00
12.00	7.30
12.35	

AR
BF
PN

CINNAMON AND COCONUT
FISH CURRY

PREP: 25 MINS
COOK: 25 MINS

2 coconuts, peeled and
   finely grated
1 litre (1¾ pints) boiling
   water olive oil
20 fresh curry leaves
2 red onions, thinly sliced
2 garlic cloves, roughly
   chopped
1 red chilli, finely sliced
2½cm (1in) piece ginger,
   peeled and finely chopped
1 tsp black mustard seeds,
   ground
2 tsp ground coriander
1 tsp coarsely ground black
   pepper
½ tsp turmeric
½ tsp fennel seeds, ground
15cm (6in) cinnamon stick,
   broken in half
1 tbsp red wine vinegar
6 courgettes, cut into 2¼cm
   (1in) wedges
4 x 175g (6oz) hake fillets,
   or other firm white fish
2 tomatoes, cut into rough
   chunks
sea salt

To serve:
steamed rice or chapattis

This recipe, from my *Dock Kitchen Cookbook*, is based on the classic Keralan fish *moilee*. It's a bit time-consuming because you have to make your own coconut milk, but is worth it. Home-made coconut milk is much more delicate and lighter than shop-bought. If you don't have the time, water-down tinned cocount milk by half.

Place the coconut in a pan or large metal bowl and pour the boiling water over it. Leave to steep while you prepare the remainder of the ingredients.

Heat a generous glug of oil in a wide, heavy-based pan over a high heat, and add the curry leaves. When they crackle, add the onions, garlic, chilli and ginger. Reduce the heat to low and cook for 10 minutes, until the onions are soft and sweet. Add the spices and continue to cook for another 5 minutes, then add the vinegar, cook for 1 minute and turn the heat down to very low.

Lay a clean tea towel in a large bowl and pour some of the coconut and water into it, quickly picking up the corners of the towel to make a bag. Squeeze as much liquid as you can through the bag. Add any remaining liquid and coconut from the pan and squeeze that too. Discard the coconut after you have squeezed it dry.

Add the coconut milk and courgettes to the onion mixture and bring to the full boil. Taste for salt and add some if necessary. Reduce the heat to medium and leave to bubble for 10 minutes. Bring back up to the boil, then add the fish and the tomatoes. Reduce the heat and simmer for a further 5–10 minutes, until the fish is cooked through. Serve with steamed rice or chapattis.

CHICKEN BRAISED WITH PRESERVED LEMONS AND CINNAMON

SERVES SIX

PREP: 10 MINS
COOK: 1½ HRS

1 x 1.5kg (3¼lb) chicken,
    jointed
olive oil, for frying
2 onions, sliced
5 garlic cloves, sliced
12cm (5in) cinnamon stick,
    broken into 4 pieces
½ tsp turmeric
1 tbsp ground coriander
1 tsp ground allspice
2 large tomatoes, cut into
    large chunks, or 1 x 400g
    tin plum tomatoes, rinsed
    and cut into quarters
40g (1½oz) raisins, soaked
    in boiling water
approx. 500ml (18fl oz)
    chicken stock
2 small whole preserved
    lemons, finely chopped
2 handfuls of coriander
    leaves, roughly chopped
sea salt and freshly ground
    black pepper

To serve:
couscous

This is one of those dishes you could happily eat once a week, so learning to make it by rote will certainly have its value. It uses small and mild preserved lemons so reduce the quantity of lemons you add to the recipe if you only have stronger ones.

Preheat the oven to 180°C/350°F/gas 4.

Season the chicken well. Heat a good glug of oil in a large, ovenproof casserole (with a lid) and brown the chicken in batches. Remove the chicken and put to one side.

Add another splash of oil to the casserole. Add the onions and cook gently for 5 minutes before adding the garlic and the spices. Continue to cook for another 10 minutes and when the onions are soft, return the chicken to the casserole and scatter the tomatoes and drained raisins over it. Pour in enough stock so it comes about halfway up the chicken, bring to the boil, put the lid on the casserole and braise in the oven for 1½ hours, until the chicken is tender and cooked through. Remove the cinnamon, then stir in the preserved lemon and the coriander leaves. Serve with couscous.

SPICED LAMB CHOPS
WITH AUBERGINE, OKRA AND TOMATO

PREP: 10 MINS
COOK: 25 MINS

1cm (½in) cinnamon stick
2 ½ tsp coriander seeds
a pinch of dried chilli flakes
12–16 lamb chops or cutlets,
   approx. 1.25kg (2½lb)
olive oil
1 aubergine, cut into 1cm
   (½in) cubes
1 red onion, finely sliced
1 green chilli, finely chopped
1 garlic clove, finely sliced
150g (5oz) okra, sliced in
   half lengthways
2 tomatoes, chopped into
   large chunks
a handful of mint leaves,
   roughly chopped
a handful of parsley leaves,
   roughly chopped
a handful of marjoram leaves
sea salt and freshly ground
   black pepper

In a pestle and mortar, bash the cinnamon stick until very fine, then add 2 teaspoons of the coriander seeds and the chilli flakes. Grind as finely as possible.

Sprinkle the lamb with a little salt, followed by a generous sprinkling of the spice mix. In a large, heavy-based frying pan, heat a good glug of oil and fry the lamb on both sides until golden, about 3 minutes each side for medium (2 minutes if using cutlets; you may have to do this in batches). Transfer to a warm plate to rest.

Meanwhile, heat a good glug of oil in a separate large frying pan and fry the aubergine until golden and soft, about 5 minutes. Remove from the pan and leave to drain on kitchen paper. Add another glug of oil to the same pan and gently fry the onion, chilli and garlic with the remaining ½ teaspoon of coriander seeds until soft and sweet, about 5 minutes, then add the okra and season well. Continue to cook for another 8 minutes, until the okra softens, then stir in the tomatoes and the aubergine and cook for another 5 minutes. Stir in the herbs and then divide the vegetables between 4 plates. Serve with the lamb chops, adding a little oil to the resting juices before pouring them over the meat.

ROLL CINNAMON   NUTMEG   STAR ANIES

CINNAMON AND SQUASH BUÑUELOS

PREP: 15 MINS
COOK: 35 MINS

400g (14oz) butternut squash,
  skin still on, cut into 3cm
  (1¼in) chunks
225g (8oz) plain flour
1 tsp baking powder
2 tsp ground cinnamon
1 heaped tbsp brown sugar
1 egg
25g (1oz) butter, melted
125ml (4½fl oz) milk
vegetable oil, for deep-frying
a large pinch of table salt
2 tbsp sugar mixed with 1 tsp
  ground cinnamon, for
  dusting

I first ate these in the street in Valencia at 3 o'clock in the morning during Las Fallas festival, when huge effigies are burned in the streets to celebrate the start of spring and lots of alcohol is drunk. Amazing as it all was, the *buñuelos* were still the highlight for me.

Preheat the oven to 200°C/400°F/gas 6.

Place the squash in a large baking tray, season with salt and cover tightly with tinfoil. Roast in the oven for 30 minutes until soft – you should be able to easily insert a table knife. Leave to cool. Remove the skin, crush with a potato masher, then push through a sieve or moulis until you have a smooth paste.

Sift the flour, baking powder, cinnamon and a large pinch of salt into a large bowl and stir in the sugar. In another bowl, beat the egg, melted butter, milk and squash paste together. Very slowly fold the dry ingredients into the wet ingredients, a tablespoonful at a time. When you have a smooth batter, cover the bowl with clingfilm, and then leave to rest in the fridge for 30 minutes.

Fill a wide, deep heavy-based pan with 8cm (3¼in) oil and place over a medium heat. Test the heat of the oil with a chunk of bread; when the bread sizzles and gently turns golden in 30 seconds, the oil's hot enough. Very carefully drop tablespoonfuls of the batter into the oil, in batches, and cook for about 5 minutes, turning once, until golden and puffed up. Remove with a slotted spoon and leave to drain on kitchen paper. Sprinkle with the cinnamon sugar before serving.

SLICED ORANGES WITH CINNAMON DATES AND HONEY

SERVES FOUR–SIX

PREP: 2 MINS

6 oranges
4 dates, stoned and
   roughly chopped
½ tsp ground cinnamon
1 tbsp honey

This recipe seems like nothing but tastes amazing. I first ate it in Tangiers and recreated it for our cinnamon-harvesting friends in Kerala to celebrate their harvest festival, Onam. Cinnamon production is simple, though time-consuming and hard work. The trunk of the cinnamon tree (a kin of laurel, like a bay tree, native to Sri Lanka) is coppiced to keep the plants small. The outer bark is scraped off and discarded from 6 month-old shoots, then the inner bark, from which the cinnamon is made, is carefully cut from the trunk. The thick, metre-long sticks are left out to dry for a few weeks until they coil into the tight quills of cinnamon. It's a process with low annual yields and slim rewards for all the hard work, but also a beautiful one that produces a wonderful and important spice.

Using a sharp knife, slice the ends off the oranges, then, standing them on one end, slice under the pith from top to bottom to remove the peel, being careful not to remove too much flesh. Slice the flesh into ½cm (¼in) rounds and divide between serving plates. Sprinkle with the cinnamon, then scatter the dates over the orange slices and drizzle with the honey.

EMMA'S CINNAMON & CASHEW NUT
LOVE CAKE

PREP: 15 MINS
COOK: 35 MINS

125g (4½oz) butter, at room
  temperature, plus extra
  for greasing
30g (1¼oz) plain flour, sifted
135g (4¾oz) semolina
300g (5oz) soft brown sugar
4 eggs, separated
4 tbsp honey
3 tbsp rose water
2 tsp ground cinnamon
½ tsp ground nutmeg
¾ tsp ground cardamom
110g (3¾oz) cashew nuts,
  very finely chopped
zest of ½ lemon
2 cinnamon sticks
200ml (⅓ pint) water
fresh or dried rose petals,
  for decorating

1 x 20cm (8in) square
  baking tin

As rich in tradition as it is in flavour, this recipe is packed with fragrant spices that work together beautifully to make an exciting, aromatic and floral cake. Historically known as Sri Lankan love cake, it's made to celebrate life and love on special occasions.

Preheat the oven to 160°C/325°F/gas 3. Butter a 20cm (8in) square baking tin.

In a bowl, cream the butter, flour and semolina together.

Add 150g (5oz) of the sugar and the egg yolks to the butter and semolina mix, along with 2 tablespoons of the honey, 2 tablespoons of the rose water, the ground spices, chopped cashews and lemon zest. Mix until thoroughly combined.

In a clean bowl, whisk the egg whites to stiff peaks then gently fold them into the mixture.

Pour the mixture evenly into the baking tin, and bake for about 30 minutes, until the cake is golden brown on top and slightly firm to the touch.

While the cake is in the oven, break the cinnamon sticks into a saucepan and combine with the remaining 2 tablespoons of honey, the resst of the sugar, a tablespoon of rose water and the water. Simmer to dissolve the sugar, reduce slightly until it's the consistency of honey, then turn off the heat and let it stand to infuse until the cake is ready.

When the cake is cooked (but still hot) and still in the tin, cut it into diamonds, strain the syrup over the cake, ensuring it covers the top of the cake and seeps into the cracks, then leave to cool in the tin. Serve sprinkled with rose petals.

RICOTTA AND CINNAMON
BREAKFAST
HOTCAKES

MAKES TEN

PREP & COOK: 10 MINS

250g (9oz) ricotta cheese
125ml (4½fl oz) milk
2 eggs, separated
100g (3½oz) plain flour, sifted
1 tsp baking powder
a pinch of sea salt
60g (2½oz) butter, mixed with
    1 tsp ground cinnamon

To serve:
honey and fresh fruit
    (optional)

A perfect breakfast whatever the weather. You'll be hugely popular if you whip these up for brunch one Sunday.

Combine the ricotta, milk and egg yolks in a bowl and mix well. Fold in the flour, baking powder and a pinch of salt and gently beat to make a smooth batter. In a separate, clean bowl, beat the egg whites until you have soft peaks, then fold them into the ricotta mixture.

In a large, heavy-based frying pan, melt a heaped teaspoon of the cinnamon butter and when it begins to foam, add tablespoons of the batter to the pan, leaving a little space between each one. When you can see bubbles breaking through the surface, turn them over. Once the pancakes are cooked and golden on both sides, transfer to a warm plate and cover with a tea towel to keep warm while you cook the remainder. Dot with the remaining cinnamon butter and serve with a drizzle of honey and some fresh fruit, if you want.

CINNAMON, SALT AND CARAMEL
ICE CREAM

PREP: 20 MINS
+30 MINS CHURNING

500ml (18fl oz) milk
500ml (18fl oz) double cream
1 vanilla pod, split
10cm (4in) cinnamon stick
8 egg yolks
250g (9oz) sugar
sea salt

We often make salt caramel ice cream at Dock Kitchen and everyone loves it. When we started adding cinnamon in too, we all loved it even more. You will need an ice cream maker for this recipe.

Heat the milk, cream, vanilla and cinnamon together in a large pan for about 10 minutes, until the mixture is just about to come to the boil.

Whisk the egg yolks with half the sugar in a large bowl and slowly pour the hot milk mixture into the bowl, whisking constantly.

Return the egg and milk mixture to the pan and cook slowly, stirring with a wooden spoon, until the mixture is thick enough to coat the back of a spoon. Leave to cool, then pass through a sieve to remove the cinnamon and vanilla pod.

Put the remaining sugar in a heavy-based pan with 125ml (4½fl oz) water and bring to the boil over a medium heat until the sugar is dark brown in colour. While it's still hot, carefully pour it over the cooling custard, stirring constantly with a whisk until any lumps of burnt sugar have dissolved. Add salt to taste, then leave to cool. Transfer to an ice cream maker and churn until frozen, following the manufacturer's instructions.

EMMA'S CINNAMON THERAPIES

Cinnamon has been used in therapies for centuries. In Kerala it is widely believed to improve brain function. An experiment at the University of Ohio appears to back up this theory. A group of students were divided into three and set study tasks. One group was given cinnamon to chew, the second was surrounded by cinnamon-scented candles, and the third had nothing. The two groups who'd been given cinnamon demonstrated better focus and quicker mental reflexes than the other group, suggesting that cinnamon might well, in fact, stimulate brain activity.

The therapeutic benefits of cinnamon were known to medieval physicians, who used it to treat coughs, sore throats and hoarseness. For cinnamon to have any therapeutic benefit it needs to be decocted – that is, the active constituents need to be to be extracted, and this is done by simmering it in boiling water for at least 5 minutes. It is often mixed with honey to make it more effective. The protective properties of cinnamon are due to a potent compound in its oil called cinnamaldehyde, which is toxic to most insects, viruses, fungi, salmonella and E. coli. For something so potent, it has relatively few side effects.

The phenols in cinnamon have been proven to inhibit the growth of bacteria, so claims as to its usefulness in preserving food may well be valid. It certainly ties in with its use in the embalming process! Studies have also shown it to be effective against Candida albicans (the fungus that causes thrush) and infection from Helicobacter pylori, the bacterium that causes gastritis and most stomach ulcers.

THE STORY OF CINNAMON

Cinnamon is native to the Malabar Coast of India, or the 'Spice Coast' as it was once known. It was, and to some extent still is the epicentre of the global spice trade. Indian cinnamon, which originated in neighbouring Sri Lanka, is one of the oldest plant species known to man. It was used in both powder and stick form by the Ancient Greeks and Egyptians as early as 2000 BC.

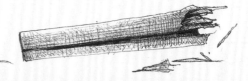

The Keralan spice trade dates back 3000 years. From Kerala it crossed the seas to Babylon and Egypt to be used for embalming and in the manufacture of perfumes and holy oils. By 600 BC, the Arabs had gained control of the spice trade and transported cinnamon, incense, and oils from the east, through the Persian Gulf, to Arabia. In the first century AD, Pliny the Elder wrote that 350 grams of cinnamon was equal in value to over 5 kilograms of silver, making it, weight per weight, 15 times more valuable than silver.

A NOTE OF WARNING

Used in high concentrations, the compound coumarin, which is found in cinnamon and other plants, has been known to cause liver and kidney damage. Measurements of coumarin in true cinnamon (0.45%) are much lower than those found in the 'fake' cinnamon known as cassia (up to 5%). In rare cases, taking cinnamon can cause contact dermatitis, which usually occurs some time after consumption and causes skin redness, itching, swelling, sweating and a sensation of burning.

MEDICINAL USES

■ One teaspoon of ground cinnamon has as much antioxidant power as one cup of pomegranate juice or half a cup of blueberries.

■ A mere teaspoonful of true cinnamon contains more than 1 per cent of the daily recommended intake of calcium, 0.5 per cent of iron and vitamin K, and 11 per cent of manganese.

■ There is some evidence that cinnamon may help slow the rate at which the stomach empties after meals, reducing the rise in blood sugar after eating. This is relevant to those with type 2 diabetes.

■ Cinnamon oil, most of which is the compound cinnamaldehyde, is an effective insect repellent and specifically used to kill mosquito larvae. The inferior, or 'fake' cinnamon – cassia – has a much higher cinnamaldehyde content than true cinnamon.

■ Cinnamon is a carminative, which means it breaks up wind in the stomach and it also combats diarrhoea and morning sickness.

■ Gargling with a mixture of honey and cinnamon powder diluted in hot water is lsaid to keep your breath fresh all day – it's cheaper than mouthwash, anyway!

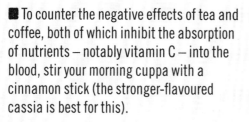

■ To counter the negative effects of tea and coffee, both of which inhibit the absorption of nutrients – notably vitamin C – into the blood, stir your morning cuppa with a cinnamon stick (the stronger-flavoured cassia is best for this).

■ Cinnamon is said to be a potent aphrodisiac.

■ It has been claimed that simply smelling cinnamon may improve cognitive function.

■ Cinnamon tea is not only delicious, it can help relieve flatulence and stomach cramps, as well as boost brain power and aid digestion.

■ Cinnamon is great for settling the stomach after a meal, which is particularly useful if you are travelling to countries where you are likely to be eating unfamiliar foods. For a simple daily cinnamon tea, dissolve half a teaspoon of freshly ground cinnamon powder in water and boil for 5 minutes.

CINNAMON LIP PLUMPER

A preparation of 3 drops of cinnamon essential oil mixed with 2 tablespoons of petroleum jelly or olive oil can be applied to fine lines around the mouth to plump out the lips, making the lines less visible. It tingles pleasantly and feels as though it's doing a wonderful job!

CINNAMON TEA FOR COLDS AND FLU

1 cinnamon stick, broken up
a few whole cloves
2½cm (1in) ginger, peeled and chopped
juice of ½ lemon
honey, to taste

Place all the ingredients in a pan and cover with 1 litre (1¾ pints) of water. Bring to the boil, then turn down the heat and simmer, covered, for 5 minutes. Strain the liquid and pour into mugs for a spicy brew.

CINNAMON OIL RUB FOR CHEST CONGESTION

Cinnamon oil is used in oil blends to ease lung problems and whooping cough.

2 drops cinnamon oil
2 drops thyme oil
2 drops lavender or hyssop oil
2 tbsp carrier oil such as almond or sunflower

Combine the oils in a dish and apply to the back and chest to ease coughing and chest congestion.

A NOTE ON KERALA

Kerala really touched my heart. I'm passionate about the use of natural and holistic healing wherever possible and it was fascinating to visit the place where Ayurvedic medicine originated. One of the oldest forms of medicine in the world, Ayurveda considers the whole body – taking into account the emotional and mental state as well as the physical manifestations of ills – instead of only fixing the surface ailments in the way that paracetamol might stop the pain of a headache rather than finding and treating its root cause.

Interestingly, cinnamon is used in every Ayurvedic medicine, as it apparently helps the body to absorb the treatment.

'ONE OF THE OLDEST FORMS OF MEDICINE IN THE WORLD, AYURVEDA CONSIDERS THE WHOLE BODY – TAKING INTO ACCOUNT THE EMOTIONAL AND MENTAL STATE AS WELL AS THE PHYSICAL MANIFESTATIONS OF ILLS'

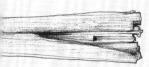

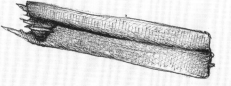

'BLACK PEPPER ISN'T JUST A FLAVOUR-ENHANCING CONDIMENT, IT CAN ALSO BE THE DOMINANT FLAVOUR'

Black pepper is the king of spices, and for good reason. It is the most common spice, making up 20 per cent of all the spices traded in the world – and with hundreds of different spices available, that's no small feat.

It seems that pepper has been somewhat taken for granted on western tables – most people probably don't even realise that it is a spice. Those little pots of pre-ground sneezing powder bear so little resemblance to freshly ground, good-quality pepper, I suppose it's no surprise that we've gone off our most ubiquitous spice.

Black pepper isn't just a flavour enhancing condiment, it can also be the dominant flavour. I'm more likely to use a lot of pepper in my cooking rather than just a little, and generally when I want something to taste of pepper itself. That's not to say I only use it in curries, I like to season things with it too, I'm just pretty heavy-handed. I love the whole corns chucked into slow-cooked lamb or grinding a generous amount to bring fiery heat to a dish, as in Emma's fantastic squid recipe. Black pepper also works surprisingly well with sweet things, from strawberries to dark chocolate. Give my brownie recipe a try and I think you'll never make them without salt and pepper again.

Black pepper is an awesome spice, and I think it's about time we gave it another look.

What home would be without pepper? Unsurprisingly, it's ranked the third most common ingredient in dishes after water and salt and is included in 95 per cent of recipes. But its status as 'king of spices' or 'master spice' gives a clue to the high profile it has maintained throughout history. A highly prized spice often referred to as 'black gold', pepper was used as commodity money to pay debts, rents, taxes or dowries. It's the world's most traded spice and one of the oldest, used for more than 4000 years and cultivated as long ago as 1000 BC.

Like many spices, pepper was the preserve of the rich: it was used in the most expensive Ancient Roman cuisine and even found stuffed in the nostrils of the Egyptian pharaoh Ramesses II as part of the mummification process. In the 16th century, sailors' pockets were sewn up to prevent them stealing this valuable cargo and, much earlier still, in AD 408, 3000 pounds of pepper was included in the ransom demand at the First Siege of Rome, along with gold, silver, tunics and dyed hides. Interestingly, the phrase 'peppercorn rent', meaning a token payment made for something in effect being given, belies this high value and may refer to the small size of the individual peppercorn itself.

Whole peppercorns can be stored for years without losing flavour or aroma, as long as the container is airtight and doesn't let in any light. It's best to grind pepper as and when needed. Although the ground spice keeps its bite, over time its flavour will diminish. A metal or glass pepper mill is preferable as wood draws out the oil in the peppercorns – a shame as there are so many beautiful wooden ones around!

PEPPER, COCONUT AND TOMATO SALAD

PREP & COOK: 30 MINS

1 tsp black peppercorns
¼ white onion
5cm (2in) piece ginger, peeled
¼ bunch coriander (leaves and
    stems), roughly chopped
1 coconut, peeled
juice of 2 limes
2 tomatoes, chopped
sea salt

This is a vibrant and unusual salad. It might seem a bit of a drag to grate a coconut but it really doesn't take very long and it's worth it. I learned to make this salad on a pepper plantation in Sri Lanka. It's a version of the sambal they make with every meal. Great on its own or with fish, or dhal and rice.

In a pestle and mortar, bash the peppercorns a couple of times to break them open, then add the onion, ginger and coriander. Bash until you have a coarse paste, then transfer to a bowl. Season with a little salt.

Using the coarse side of a grater, grate in the coconut and stir well so it absorbs all the flavours. Squeeze in the lime juice and stir in the tomatoes before serving.

SPICY PEPPER SCRAMBLED EGGS

SERVES FOUR

PREP & COOK: 15 MINS

25g (1oz) butter
1 white onion, finely chopped
a pinch of sea salt
½ garlic clove, finely chopped
a pinch of turmeric
½ tsp ground cumin
½ tsp coriander seeds, ground
½ tsp coarsely ground black
   pepper
1 small tomato, diced
a handful of spinach leaves,
   finely chopped
6 eggs, beaten with a pinch
   of salt
1 green chilli, finely sliced
a small handful of coriander
   leaves

To serve:
toasted bread

This Indian version of scrambled eggs makes an excellent start to the day. It may sound like it might be a little challenging first thing in the morning, but try it – it really isn't and is much more interesting than everyday scrambled eggs.

In a large, heavy-based pan over a medium heat, melt the butter and fry the onion with a pinch of salt until golden. Add the garlic and spices and continue to cook for another minute before adding half the tomato and the handful of spinach.

Pour in the eggs, turn the heat down slightly and cook, stirring, until the eggs are cooked to your liking. Stir in the remaining tomato and the sliced green chilli and tear in the coriander leaves before serving with toast.

PEPPER AND CHEESE PASTA

SERVES FOUR

PREP & COOK: 15 MINS

500g (1¼lb) bucatini or
   spaghetti
75g (3oz) butter
a generous pinch of coarsely
   ground black pepper
a handful of grated pecorino
a couple of handfuls of
   grated Parmesan
sea salt

This is the classic Roman pasta *Cacio e Pepe* —
so few ingredients but amazing flavour.

Bring a large pan of salted water to the boil and cook
the pasta according to the packet instructions.

In a large, heavy-based pan (one that's big enough to
hold the cooked pasta later) over a low heat, gently heat
the butter with a generous pinch of black pepper until
the butter is melted, but not foaming.

Drain the pasta, reserving half a cup of cooking liquid.
Toss the pasta in the melted butter until all the strands
are coated, then add the cheeses and a little cooking
liquid, and stir until well combined. Taste for seasoning
and add more of the pasta cooking liquid if the pasta
becomes stiff; you want a thick, glossy sauce coating
all the pasta.

EMMA'S GRILLED SQUID WITH ZINGY BLACK PEPPERCORN SAUCE

SERVES FOUR

PREP & COOK: 25 MINS

4 smallish squid, cleaned

For the sauce:
1 tbsp fish sauce
a pinch of salt
2 tsp palm sugar
    (or light brown sugar)
juice of 1 lime
2 tbsp freshly ground
    black pepper

For the salad (if using):
chopped vegetables such
    as radish, cucumber,
    carrot, spring onions

The key to this dish is not to overcook the squid. You can serve the sauce as a dip, or add salad and toss the squid and salad with the sauce.

Preheat the grill to high or heat a griddle pan or barbecue.

Cut the body of each squid down one side and open them out (reserve the tentacles). Score the inside of the flesh in a criss-cross fashion with a knife.

Combine all the sauce ingredients in a bowl.

Grill or griddle the squid on a high heat for no more than 1–2 minutes each side, until lightly charred. Repeat with the tentacles. Do not cook for longer or the squid will get rubbery.

Serve the squid with the dipping sauce, or toss the squid and salad together and use the sauce as a dressing.

SALT AND PEPPER QUAIL WITH HOT AND SOUR DIPPING SAUCE

PREP: 20 MINS
COOK: 20 MINS

1 egg white
250ml (8fl oz) sparkling water
150g (5oz) plain flour, plus
    extra for coating
3 tsp coarsely ground black
    pepper, plus extra for
    serving
4 quails, spatchcocked and
    cut in half lengthways
vegetable oil, for frying
sea salt

*For the hot and sour
    dipping sauce:*
2.5cm (1in) piece ginger,
    peeled and roughly chopped
½ garlic clove
½ bird's-eye chilli
1 tbsp fish sauce, plus
    extra if needed
a pinch of sugar, plus
    extra if needed
juice of 1 lime

Quails may seem a bit fancy, but really they're just like miniature chickens but with a slightly richer meat. They're straightforward to cook and super-versatile – happy to be a starter or main and they work well alongside loads of different flavours. You can also use poussin or partridge in this recipe if you find quail hard to find. If you don't fancy the fuss of deep frying, you can roast the quail simply with a little salt for 15 minutes at 220°C/425°F/gas 7.

In a clean bowl, whisk the egg white until it forms stiff peaks. In a separate bowl, whisk the water into the flour and beat until you have a paste. Fold in the egg white and season with a pinch of salt and the black pepper.

In a pestle and mortar, bash the ginger, garlic and chilli to a thick paste, then stir in the fish sauce, sugar and lime juice. Add a little more fish sauce or sugar, if necessary, until it has a nice balance. Transfer to a dipping bowl.

Heat 10cm (4in) of oil in a large, deep, heavy-based pan over a medium heat. Test the heat of the oil with a chunk of bread; if the bread sizzles and turns golden in 30 seconds, the oil is hot enough. Coat the quails in a little flour, shake off any excess, then dip in the batter and very carefully lower into the oil. Fry until golden (you may have to do this in batches), about 10 minutes. Remove with a slotted spoon and leave to drain and rest for a minute or so on kitchen paper. Generously sprinkle the quails with sea salt and a little extra pepper before serving with the dipping sauce.

PEPPER AND HORSERADISH

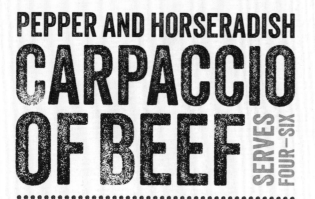

CARPACCIO OF BEEF

SERVES FOUR–SIX

PREP & COOK: 10 MINS + RESTING

700g (1½lb) beef fillet
3 tsp coarsely ground
    black pepper
extra-virgin olive oil
a couple of handfuls
    of rocket, chopped
3cm (1¼in) stick fresh
    horseradish, peeled
sea salt

I learned to make carpaccio this way at River Café. As a starter or light lunch it's a great illustration of how brilliant beef is with pepper.

Place the beef on a chopping board and season it all over with salt and the black pepper so the entire surface of the meat is well covered in seasoning.

Put a large, heavy-based pan over a high heat and add a splash of oil. When it's very hot, add the meat and fry for 1 minute, turning it constantly so that all sides are seared. Remove the meat with tongs and leave to rest and cool on a wooden board. When cool, chill in the fridge for at least 20 minutes so it's easier to slice.

Slice the beef thinly with a sharp knife, flattening each slice as much as possible with the flat side of the knife. Divide the beef between plates and season very lightly. Scatter the rocket and grate the horseradish over the beef, and finish with a good drizzle of olive oil.

DEEP-FRIED BLACK PEPPER TOFU

PREP & COOK: 10 MINS

1 x 350g packet silken tofu,
    drained on kitchen paper
2 tbsp cornflour, rice flour
    or plain flour
vegetable oil, for frying
6 garlic cloves, peeled
10 spring onions, trimmed and
    cut into 3cm (1¼in) lengths
1 heaped tsp black
    peppercorns, coarsely
    ground
a good pinch of sea salt

To serve:
steamed rice

This is a classic Malaysian recipe. It calls for lots of pepper, and needs it. I didn't like tofu before I lived in Japan, but walking up to see the tofu man in the early morning and having a warm glass of soya milk while waiting for the curds to separate, quickly converted me to this wonderfully versatile ingredient. This dish is best served hot as it gets soggy quickly.

Cut the tofu into 2cm (¾in) cubes and toss in the flour to coat, shaking off any excess.

Heat 2cm (¾in) of oil in a large, deep, heavy-based pan over a medium heat. Test the heat of the oil with a chunk of bread; if the bread sizzles and turns golden in 30 seconds, the oil is hot enough. Fry the tofu in batches, turning it regularly until golden. Remove with a slotted spoon and drain on kitchen paper.

Get a wok or frying pan nice and hot over a high heat and add a good spoonful of oil. Fry the garlic cloves for a few moments until they turn golden, stirring them and moving them around constantly. Add the spring onion and continue to cook, stirring, until it begins to soften. Stir in the tofu and cook for 1 minute until it is heated through and then sprinkle in the ground peppercorns and a good pinch of salt. Continue to cook for another minute, then take off the heat and serve immediately with steamed rice.

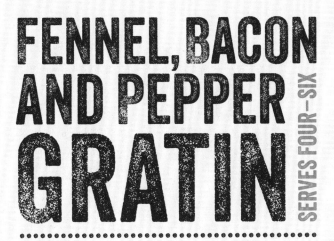

FENNEL, BACON AND PEPPER GRATIN

SERVES FOUR–SIX

PREP: 15 MINS
COOK: 40–45 MINS

200ml (⅓ pint) double cream
3 garlic cloves, peeled
4 large fennel bulbs, tough
   outer layers discarded
   and green fronds reserved
olive oil
6 rashers smoked streaky
   bacon or pancetta, cut into
   ½cm (¼in) pieces
75g (3oz) dried breadcrumbs
¼ bunch thyme, leaves picked
a small handful of parsley
   leaves, roughly chopped
15 black peppercorns, roughly
   crushed
sea salt and freshly ground
   black pepper

This is perfect as a side or a simple supper in itself.

Preheat the oven to 180°C/350°F/gas 4. In a pan, gently heat the cream with a pinch of salt and the garlic. Simmer for 25 minutes, making sure it doesn't boil over.

Meanwhile, cut the fennel into 12 wedges, making sure you cut through the root without slicing all the way through, so that the pieces hold together. Bring a pan of salted water to the boil and blanch the fennel until soft (you should be able to easily insert a table knife), about 5–10 minutes. Drain and sit the fennel in an ovenproof dish that holds it snugly. Season well with ground black pepper.

Add a little oil to a frying pan and gently fry the bacon until crisp, then remove with a slotted spoon, keeping the fat in the pan. Scatter the bacon over the fennel, then pour the hot cream over the top.

Combine the breadcrumbs, thyme, parsley and fennel fronds in the bacon pan and toss well so that they're coated in fat. Use to evenly cover the fennel, then sprinkle the crushed black pepper on top. Bake for 15–20 minutes until golden and bubbling. Leave to cool for a moment before serving.

GREEN PEPPERCORN

PRAWNS

SERVES FOUR–SIX

PREP & COOK: 10 MINS

groundnut oil, for frying
2cm (¾in) piece ginger, peeled
 and finely chopped
4 garlic cloves, finely chopped
20 large whole raw prawns,
 unpeeled
2 tbsp green pickled or fresh
 peppercorns
a handful of fresh kaffir lime
 leaves, sliced into strips
2 tbsp oyster sauce
1 tbsp soy sauce
2 tbsp fish sauce
2 tomatoes, finely diced
a handful of coriander
 leaves, roughly chopped
juice of 1 lime, to serve

This is a version of the amazing Kampot Green Pepper Crab we had in Cambodia. It is one of my all-time favourite dishes. This variation with prawns works well as it's hard to get soft-shell crabs. Thai shops sell fresh green peppercorns on the stem, or you can buy them brined in little jars in the supermarket.

Get a wok nice and hot over a very high heat and add some oil. Add the ginger and garlic and cook, stirring continuously, until the garlic just begins to colour. Add the prawns, peppercorns and kaffir lime leaves and stir well to combine.

When the prawns begin to change colour, stir in the oyster, soy and fish sauces and cook until the prawns have turned pink completely. Stir in the tomatoes and the coriander leaves. Taste, and add a little more fish sauce if necessary. Serve with a good squeeze of lime juice.

EMMA'S BLACK PEPPER CHICKEN CURRY SERVES FOUR

PREP TIME: 15 MINS + MARINATING
COOK: 30 MINS

1 x 1.5kg (3¼lb) whole chicken, skinned and jointed, or 8 chicken thighs, skinned
4 tsp freshly cracked Tellicherry or Kampot black peppercorns
1 tsp turmeric
juice of ½ lemon
1 tsp sea salt
3 white onions, half thinly sliced and half roughly chopped
3 garlic cloves, crushed
3cm (1¼in) piece ginger, peeled and finely chopped or grated
olive oil

To serve:
steamed rice
chapattis
salad

Peppery and nutty with a kick, this curry demonstrates the different levels of flavour that pepper can bring to a dish. Here, it is toasted and cooked into the sauce and then sprinkled on at the end for extra aroma and heat.

Put the chicken in a large dish. In a small bowl, combine a quarter of the black pepper, the turmeric, lemon juice and a pinch of salt, then rub all over the chicken and leave to marinate, covered, for a few hours.

Blend the roughly chopped onions with the garlic and ginger to make a paste.

Toast the remaining pepper in a hot, dry pan until there's a delicious nutty, toasty scent and the pepper begins to smoke. Shake the pan so the pepper doesn't burn.

Heat a good glug of oil in a heavy-based frying pan (one with a lid) and fry the sliced onions until they turn soft and golden. Add the onion paste and continue frying until all the liquid has evaporated and the onion is starting to brown.

Add the toasted pepper (reserve a generous pinch for later) and the chicken including all the marinade juices, 300ml (½ pint) water and ½ tsp salt.

Bring to the boil, cover and simmer for 30 minutes, or until the chicken is cooked through – add a splash more water if the curry gets too thick.

Serve the curry sprinkled with the reserved toasted black pepper, alongside some boiled rice, warmed chapattis and the salad.

THREE-TIMES-COOKED LAMB CURRY

SERVES 4–6

WITH BLACK PEPPER AND COCONUT RICE

PREP: 45 MINS
COOK: 3 HRS

Stage one:
olive oil
1 x 2kg (4½lb) lamb or mutton
    shoulder, deboned, excess
    fat trimmed and meat cut
    into 5cm (2in) chunks
6 whole cloves
10 green cardamom pods
15cm (6in) cinnamon stick
½ tbsp turmeric
3 dried chillies
20 black peppercorns
2 big handfuls of curry leaves
sea salt

Stage two:
olive oil
2 red onions, finely sliced
15cm (6in) piece ginger,
    unpeeled and coarsely
    grated
4 tbsp ground coriander
15cm (6in) stick cinnamon
5 dried chillies
15 whole cloves
15 green cardamom pods,
    seeded and shells discarded

This is a version of a classic Keralan curry. The three stages help to build flavour and give the meat a great texture. It's a little time-consuming but fun to make and tastes amazing. The whole peppercorns soften as they're slow cooked and are really delicious to eat.

Preheat the oven to 140°C/275°F/gas 1. For the first stage, heat a good glug of oil in a heavy-based frying pan (with a lid). Season the lamb with salt and fry in batches until golden. Remove with a slotted spoon to a deep roasting tin and scatter the remainder of the stage one ingredients over the lamb. Add enough water to just cover the meat and cook in the oven for 2 hours. Drain the lamb and strain the braising stock, reserving 125ml (4½fl oz).

For the second stage, heat a little oil in the frying pan used in stage one, and fry the onions, ginger and spices over a medium heat, until the onions are soft (about 15 minutes). Stir in the lamb, then put the lid on the pan and cook over a low heat for 20 minutes.

For the third stage, get another large, heavy-based pan and some more oil. Turn the heat up nice and high and fry the mustard seeds, chilli and curry leaves for 20 seconds until the seeds pop and the leaves are translucent. Add the peppercorns and transfer the lamb to the pan. Fry, stirring, until the lamb is golden on all sides (about 5 minutes). Add the tomatoes and cook for another 3 minutes. Skim the reserved braising stock and pour into the pan. Turn the heat down to medium and leave to bubble away, uncovered, until the liquid has reduced by half.

272
PEPPER
LARGE
PLATES

Stage three:
olive oil
1 tbsp black mustard seeds
1 dried chilli
10 curry leaves
1 tbsp black peppercorns,
   just cracked
2 tomatoes, roughly chopped

For the coconut rice:
25g (1oz) butter
200g (7oz) basmati rice, soaked
   for 1 hour and drained
1 x 400ml tin coconut milk
a pinch of table salt

To serve:
lime pickle (optional)

Recipe continued

In another large, heavy-based pan (with a lid),
melt the butter and stir in the drained rice. Cook
over a low heat for 3 minutes, stirring gently so
as not to break up the rice.

Meanwhile, in a separate, clean pan, bring the
coconut milk to the boil with a pinch of salt, then
pour it over the rice. Put the lid on and leave to boil
on a high heat for 3 minutes, then turn the heat
down to low for 6 minutes. Turn the heat off and
leave to steam for at least 10 minutes. Serve with
the lamb and a little lime pickle if you like.

PEPPER RULES

WHAT TO USE WHEN

There are a few different types of pepper, all from different places. The best is probably the Kampot we ate in Cambodia, or from Pondicherry in India. Pepper from these regions is really special, but, unless you become a real pepper-head, there's no need to seek them out – all pepper is fantastic when freshly ground.

Green pepper is slowly becoming more readily available, either in brine or fresh on the vine from Thai and Vietnamese shops. It's simply un-dried black pepper and it's really extraordinary. You can use it almost like a vegetable. It's the finest part of one of my favourite dishes: Kampot pepper crab (see page 268 for the recipe). It's just a simple stir-fry, but one of those dishes that is much greater than the sum of its parts.

White pepper is just black pepper without the skin, and without much of the flavour too, although there are a few Chinese recipes that call for its slightly different flavour and where it works well.

Pink pepper is another beast entirely and, like white pepper, not one I am particularly fond of – the pretty pink corns seem to offer so much, yet deliver so little. It's a different plant to black pepper – a species called Peruvian pepper. Occasionally you come across red pepper. The deep, maroon-coloured corn is the fully-ripe version of black pepper and has a sweetness and delicacy that can be really appealing.

STORAGE

The outer layer of the black peppercorn contains important odour-compounds which give citrus, wood, and floral notes. The spiciness comes from piperine. All of these oils are lost through evaporation and damaged by strong light, so airtight storage out of direct light preserves pepper's spice and flavour longer.

PEPPER QUICK FIXES

- Sprinkle over fruit before grilling

- Spice up gingerbread or homemade biscuits by adding ground pepper to the mixture before baking

PEPPER SPICE BLEND

2-parts ground black peppercorns
2-parts ground allspice
1-part ground cinnamon
1-part salt
½-part dried thyme
½-part ground nutmeg
½-part ground cloves

Uses: spicy and very warming so perfect for winter; works well with meat – add to stews or combine with minced chilli and garlic to marinade pork, chicken or beef before grilling, frying or barbecuing.

PEPPERY STEAK BAGUETTE

SERVES TWO

PREP & COOK: 10 MINS

3cm (1¼in) piece ginger
1 garlic clove
fish sauce
2 x 150g (5oz) minute steaks
1 tsp coarsely ground black
    peppercorns
olive oil
1 small baguette, halved
    and sliced horizontally
2 coriander sprigs
a handful of radishes, sliced
1 carrot, thinly sliced with
    a peeler
¼ cucumber, thinly sliced
    with a peeler
½ red chilli, thinly sliced
sea salt and freshly ground
    black pepper

To serve:
juice of 1 lime

I made this when we were in Cambodia. Baguettes are found all over south-east Asia and the Cambodians are big fans of French food. This recipe is a sort of Cambodian version of a French steak sandwich.

In a pestle and mortar, crush the ginger and garlic into a paste and stir in a little fish sauce. Pour the marinade over the steaks and rub in so the meat is evenly coated. Leave to marinate in the fridge for at least 1 hour.

Put a frying pan or griddle pan over a high heat. Sprinkle the meat with some salt and the ground black pepper and drizzle with oil. When the pan is nice and hot, add the steaks and press them down with a wooden spoon to make sure all of the meat is in contact with the pan. Cook for 1 minute on each side. Leave to rest for 3 minutes, before slicing the steak thickly and arranging it in the baguette halves. Push in the coriander and sliced vegetables, sprinkle with the red chilli and squeeze in the lime juice before serving.

BLACK PEPPER AND STRAWBERRY RIPPLE ICE CREAM

SERVES SIX

PREP: 15 MINS + 30 MINS CHURNING

500ml (18fl oz) milk
500ml (18fl oz) double cream
20 black peppercorns
10 egg yolks
250g (9oz) sugar

For the ripple:
100g (4oz) strawberries,
    hulled and halved
50g (2oz) sugar
3 tsp coarsely ground
    black pepper

This is a play on the classic pairing of pepper and strawberry. This recipe works best if you use an ice cream maker.

In a large pan over a medium heat, warm the milk, cream and peppercorns together until just about to boil, about 10 minutes.

In a large bowl, whisk together the egg yolks and sugar, and slowly pour the hot milk mixture over them, whisking constantly.

Return the egg and milk mixture to the pan and cook slowly, stirring with a wooden spoon until thick enough to coat the back of a spoon. Leave to cool, then pass through a sieve to remove peppercorns. Transfer to an ice cream maker and churn until frozen, following the manufacturer's instructions.

Meanwhile, mash the strawberries with the sugar, then use a spatula to push them through a sieve so you have a smooth purée. Stir in the ground pepper. Just before serving, swirl the black pepper and strawberry purée through the ice cream.

SALT AND PEPPER HAZELNUT BROWNIES

MAKES SIXTEEN

PREP: 15 MINS
COOK: 20–25 MINS

170g (5¾oz) dark chocolate
(70 per cent cocoa solids),
roughly broken up
120g (4½oz) butter
3 eggs
150g (5oz) sugar
1 tsp table salt
3 tsp coarsely ground black
peppercorns
100g (3½oz) toasted
hazelnuts, half roughly
chopped and half left whole
½ tsp sea salt

1 x approx. 28cm (11in)
brownie tin or shallow
baking tin

Adding salt and pepper to brownies makes them a bit more
adult and adds an interesting savoury element that works
really well with dark chocolate. This recipe uses no flour,
so these are a perfect gluten-free treat.

Preheat the oven to 180°C/350°F/gas 4. Line the brownie
or baking tin with baking paper.

Melt the chocolate and butter in a glass or metal bowl
over a pan of barely simmering water (make sure the
water doesn't touch the bowl), stirring a couple of times,
until the chocolate is just melted and smooth.

In a separate mixing bowl, use an electric whisk (you can
do this by hand but it will take a while) to beat the eggs,
sugar, salt and 1 teaspoon of the coarsely ground pepper
until very light and fluffy and tripled in volume. Sift in
the flour and whisk to combine.

Stir in the melted chocolate mixture and, when it is
incorporated, fold in the hazelnuts. Pour into the tin
and sprinkle with the remaining pepper and the sea salt.
Bake for 20–25 minutes, until the surface is firm but
gives a little when you touch it.

Leave to cool in the tin before cutting into squares. The
brownies will keep in an airtight container for 2–3 days.

BLACK CHERRIES
IN RED WINE AND PEPPER WITH
SWEET YOGHURT

PREP & COOK:
15 MINS + 2 HRS COOLING

50g (2oz) black peppercorns,
  lightly bashed
500ml (18 fl oz) Pinot Noir,
  or other peppery wine
  such as Valpolicella
150g (5oz) sugar
400g (14oz) black cherries,
  stoned and halved

For the sweet yoghurt:
450ml (¾ pint) Greek-style
  yoghurt
3 tbsp icing sugar

These are even better the next day when all the
flavours have been absorbed by the cherries.

Place the peppercorns in a small piece of muslin
or a clean scrap of old t-shirt material and fold up
and tie the sides to make a bag.

Pour the wine into a large pan along with the bag
of peppercorns and the sugar. Bring to the boil, then
turn the heat down to medium and leave to bubble for
10 minutes. Add the cherries, then take off the heat and
leave to infuse and cool for 2 hours. Remove the bag
of peppercorns, checking that none have escaped,
and discard.

To make the sweet yoghurt, pour the yoghurt into
a bowl and stir in the icing sugar. Serve the cherries,
either reheated or cold, with the yoghurt.

DANISH BLACK PEPPER CHRISTMAS COOKIES

MAKES ONE HUNDRED

100ml (3½fl oz) honey
50ml (2fl oz) treacle
225g (8oz) soft brown sugar
2 tbsp ground ginger
1 tsp ground black
  peppercorns
175g (6oz) butter
150ml (¼ pint) double cream
½ tsp baking soda
700g (1½lb) plain wheat flour,
  plus a little extra for dusting
a pinch of sea salt

For the icing:
300g (11oz) icing sugar

Based on a recipe by my friend Trina Hanneman, these cookies make great presents at Christmas and seem to last for ages. You could add other spices such as cloves, cardamom or cinnamon if you wanted to.

In a large saucepan, combine the honey, treacle, sugar, ginger, pepper and butter and cook gently over a low heat, stirring until the butter has just melted. Take off the heat and stir in the cream. Leave to cool slightly, then transfer to a mixing bowl. Sift over the baking soda, flour and salt and carefully fold into the butter mixture to form a dough.

On a lightly floured surface, knead the dough until smooth, then wrap in clingfilm and leave to chill in the fridge overnight.

The following day, preheat the oven to 200°C/400°F/gas 6, and line one or more baking trays with baking paper. Roll out the dough to 1cm (½in) thick and cut into cookie shapes – a selection of different shapes and sizes is nice. Collect the offcuts and continue to roll and cut until you've used up the dough. Any excess can be frozen.

Place the cookies, spaced out, on the baking trays and bake for about 8 minutes. Transfer to a wire rack to cool. When cool, decorate with a little icing. Add a little water to the icing sugar and mix until you have a smooth (but not too runny) paste. Spread or drizzle over the cookies and leave to set before serving. These cookies will keep for a week in an airtight container.

SWEET BLACK PEPPER TEA

PREP: 5 MINS

40ml (1½fl oz) milk
3 green cardamom pods,
    crushed
½ tbsp black peppercorns
1 tbsp sugar
2cm (¾in) piece ginger, peeled
    and sliced into thin rounds
3 whole cloves
6cm (2½in) cinnamon stick,
    broken in half
2 tsp loose black tea leaves
400ml (14fl oz) boiling water

This is the classic masala chai of north India. Vary the spices as you see fit. It always needs sugar, though.

In a pan, bring the milk, cardamom and peppercorns to the boil and cook for 3 minutes. Add the sugar and stir until dissolved.

Meanwhile, place the ginger, cloves, cinnamon and loose tea in a large jug and pour the boiling water over it. Leave to brew for 1 minute.

Strain the tea into a teapot and pour in the milk. Taste, and add more sugar if desired. Pour into cups from a bit of a height to create some froth.

MY BLACK PEPPER BLOODY MARY

MAKES SIX

PREP: 5 MINS

1 tomato, roughly chopped,
    or 300ml (½ pint) fresh
    tomato juice
80g (3¼oz) dried tamarind
    pulp
2½ tsp fish sauce, or to taste
10 coriander leaves, chopped
4 pinches coarsely ground
    black peppercorns
6 dashes of Tabasco
2 pinches table salt
70ml (2¾fl oz) tequila
ice

To serve:
fish sauce
coarsely ground black pepper
150ml (¼ pint) beer (optional)

Using fresh tomato gives this a cleaner taste and makes a shorter cocktail, but if you like your Bloody Marys long, just replace it with tomato juice and serve in a tall glass. I like to follow my Bloody Marys with a beer chaser, but I don't expect everyone will want to!

In a cocktail shaker, muddle the tomato (or tomato juice) and tamarind together until you have a paste, then add the remainder of the ingredients and plenty of ice. Shake really hard for about 1 minute. Taste and add more fish sauce if you want.

Rub the rims of each glass with a little fish sauce and roll them in some black pepper.

Pour the cocktail into the glasses and divide the beer between 6 shot glasses. Serve the Bloody Mary, followed by the beer as a chaser.

289
PEPPER
SWEET
THINGS

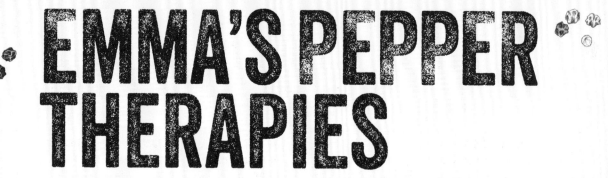

EMMA'S PEPPER THERAPIES

Black pepper is one of the few medicines Buddhist monks are allowed to carry with them because of its powerful therapeutic qualities. Pepper aids digestion and can help relieve problems such as flatulence, constipation, diarrhoea, wind and loss of appetite. The compound piperine, found in pepper, stimulates the taste buds. This triggers increased production of hydrochloric acid and digestive enzymes in the stomach, which improves digestion. Many cultures around the world have mixed pepper with castor oil, ghee and even cow's urine to produce digestive aids.

Another benefit of pepper is in helping to relieve symptoms of colds and coughs. The hot flavour of pepper stimulates membranes inside the nose and throat to secrete a lubricating substance that acts as an expectorant to help drain mucus from the lungs. Applied externally as a massage oil pepper oil is said to increase circulation and bring warmth to an area. This in turn helps to flush away toxins that are often a cause of sore muscles. It can also help in the treatment of pain relief and is often found in remedies for rheumatism and arthritis, tired limbs and stiffness, and in warming liniment formulas for aches, pains and circulation in muscles and joints.

In Cambodia we learned that pepper is used widely by new mothers, not only for its antibacterial properties, but also to build the mother's strength and vitality after childbirth and help her regain her figure. And arguably its most exciting benefit for us in the West – pepper is said to help reduce cellulite!

THE STORY OF PEPPER
Native to south-east Asia, pepper has been used in Indian cooking as far back as the 2nd century BC and was a key crop on India's Malabar coast. Used in Egypt and Ancient Greece, it was a popular ingredient in cooking by Rome's most exclusive cooks and remained hugely expensive well into the Middle Ages. In 1494, when the Portuguese signed the Treaty of Tordesillas after opening up the spice route to India, they were granted exclusive rights to the half of the world where black pepper originated.

A NOTE OF WARNING
Take care when using black pepper oil on the skin – it must be diluted properly in a carrier oil such as almond or olive oil, as used on its own it can burn. Never take black pepper oil internally. Avoid using during pregnancy.

MEDICINAL USES

■ Using pepper in meals may significantly increase the body's absorption of nutrients from the food.

■ Pepper can help fight tooth decay and provide relief from toothache, so it's great for dental hygiene.

■ Inhaling pepper oil mixed with eucalyptus or marjoram can relieve sinusitis.

■ Pepper is great for a cold: a tea made of strong black pepper and mint can help clear up chest and lung infections; and chewing peppercorns can help reduce throat inflammation.

■ In Indian medicine, eating pepper is thought to increase sweating, which can lower the body temperature during high fever.

■ Black pepper can boost circulation. Herbalists regard pepper as a stimulant and, taken internally, it can increase the metabolism and therefore help dieters lose weight more efficiently. Used regularly, black pepper can help improve the functioning of the digestive system and support elimination via the bowels, which in turn is thought to help reduce the bumpy skin created by cellulite. Use black pepper essential oil in a scrub along with ginger and grapefruit oils to improve circulation and help the breakdown of cellulite.

■ Mothers in Cambodia swear by pepper's antibacterial properties. They believe that putting ground black pepper in the belly button of a newborn baby dries it out and helps it heal.

■ Ants hate pepper! Try sprinkling ground pepper on the floor to deter them, or dilute ½ teaspoon freshly ground pepper in 1 litre (1¾ pints) warm water and spray on garden plants or pot plants to rid them of ants.

■ A weekly treatment of 1g ground black pepper mixed with 100g (3½oz) plain unsweetened yoghurt applied smoothly over the head and hair for 1 hour, followed by a mild shampoo, is said to help restore black hair colour.

■ Having trouble giving up smoking? Inhaling the vapour of black pepper extract may help with some withdrawal symptoms.

■ Pepper is a great essential oil to blend with other fragrances as it is classed as a 'middle note' oil which has a balancing effect and therefore won't compete too strongly with other scents. Black pepper oil blends well with other warming oils like clove and it provides an effective balance to citrus scents such as lemon and lime, and luxurious, rich scents such as frankincense.

BLACK PEPPER ROOM FRAGRANCE

The hot, spicy scent of black pepper essential oil is warming to cold bodies and even cold hearts; it's thought to help people 'in a rut' express love and emotion and release emotional tension, and its warming effect is wonderful for helping the home feel more cosy. Simply heat black pepper oil in an aromatherapy diffuser. The warmth created by the black pepper oil in the room can also help break up mucus in the lungs and it works as a mild decongestant and expectorant to help fight colds, flu, bronchitis and catarrh.

BLACK PEPPER PEST DETERRENT

Black pepper is an effective deterrent to insects and animals like cats and dogs. A solution of ½ teaspoon freshly ground pepper to 1.2 litres (2 pints) of warm water sprayed on plants can be toxic to ants, potato bugs, silverfish and even roaches and moths, as well as keeping cats out of your garden. A sprinkling of ground pepper can also deter insects from making a home in your house.

BLACK PEPPER MASSAGE OR BATH OIL

A solution of 1 tablespoon carrier oil such as sweet almond or olive oil (a mixture of primrose and almond oils works well on dry or mature skins) and 3 drops of black pepper essential oil can help to relieve muscle complaints and improve circulation. It also reduces the build-up of lactic acid in exercising muscles, which helps prevent soreness later. This solution can also be rubbed into tender joints to help soothe arthritic pain and stiffness, making it a good blend for runners, cyclists and other sport enthusiasts who suffer from muscular complaints.

BLACK PEPPER SCRUB

Warming, cleansing and exfoliating, this will pep up your skin, leaving it smooth and revived.

grapeseed /sunflower/ olive oil
8 tbsp of sugar or coarse salt
1 tbsp freshly crushed pepper
a few drops of grapefruit or juniper oil to help with the toning effect, or your favourite essential oil added for fragrance

Mix the essential oil with a few tablespoons of carrier oil (grapeseed etc.) Combine the sugar or salt and pepper, pour over enough oil to make a loose paste. If it is too runny, add more sugar and stir together. Scrub on to dry skin in a vigorous circular motion beginning with hands and feet and working towards the heart for the maximum circulation boost. If you're feeling really brave wash it off in a cold shower. Not for the faint hearted!

The remaining scrub will keep in an airtight jar for ages as oil and sugar are both preservatives. For extra zing zest 1 lemon into the scrub and store in the fridge.

Alternatively, a few drops of black pepper oil and a few drops of grapefruit oil in some carrier oil make a refreshing and stimulating bath oil.

A NOTE ON CAMBODIA

Cambodia felt like a country pregnant with beauty and tragedy. Like a phoenix rising from the ashes, its physical beauty was matched only by the spirit of its inhabitants, and it was humbling to experience such a sense of strength and positivity among people who have suffered so greatly.

I was intrigued to learn about the ancient black pepper rituals performed to this day by women in cities and country alike. Black pepper is used to warm new mothers, both from the inside via food and from the outside via the heat created as pepper is thrown on to fires that burn underneath the mother's bed for three whole days after the birth. It's thought that the pepper drives out toxins, helping to restore the immune system, strength and life-force in new mothers. Many women testify to the positive effects and I was repeatedly told that 'baby blues' do not exist in Cambodia because of the pepper.

I LOVE the idea of being warmed and nourished in this way after giving birth – it's just what a new mum needs.

'BLACK PEPPER IS USED TO WARM NEW MOTHERS, BOTH FROM THE INSIDE VIA FOOD AND FROM THE OUTSIDE VIA THE HEAT CREATED AS PEPPER IS THROWN ON TO FIRES THAT BURN UNDERNEATH THE MOTHER'S BED FOR THREE WHOLE DAYS AFTER THE BIRTH'

COOK'S NOTES

We always find the best ingredients are the most beautiful. Whole spices, vividly coloured and without any dust; sparkly, beautiful wild fish; dry-aged meat with a good fat content. Just trust your instincts and build relationships with your butcher, fishmonger and greengrocer.

Eggs are free-range organic and large

Butter is unsalted unless otherwise specified

Milk is whole and organic

Our meat is free-range and organic, rare breed

Fish is MSC-certified

Vegetables are medium-sized and organic

We like to drain and rinse our tinned tomatoes — always buy the most expensive you can find

We recommend washing all vegetables and fruit before use

Parsley is flat leaf

Sugar is golden caster sugar

Flour is plain

We recommend sea salt flakes and freshly ground black pepper

INDEX

This book is dedicated to our boys, Mateo and Sam; may they see and experience the world as we have, in all its vibrant colour and flavour.

A NOTE FROM THE AUTHORS

For all your hard work, creative talents, sense of the ridiculous and faith in us, a big, big thank you to Nicola Gooch (you rock); Caroline Ross Pirie and the Alchemy TV team; Caroline McArthur and the publishing team at Square Peg; Andrew Jackson, Karoline Copping, Shirley Patton and Jay Hunt from Channel 4. Thank you to Jason Lowe and Joe Woodhouse our brilliant photographers; sound man Steve Bowden who's heard it all; Olympic camera man Danny Rohrer who's seen it all; and Toby Everett, the Human Hoover, who has literally eaten it all; all our Spice Trip mothers (our lovely production team and directors) who have looked after us as we bumbled around the world; the food shoot and Mexico teams – Chris Titus-King, Ryan Chandler and Paul Arton – we love you Spice Trip crew! Thanks to all the wonderful, inspiring people we have met, who contributed their knowledge and stories along the way, and thank you to Charlie Parsons for making the Spice Trip possible.

A special note from Alchemy TV: Thanks to Stevie and Emma for their brilliance and joie de vivre; to Nicky, Sam 'Sunboy', Baby Parle, Sam Wylde, Mateo, Jenny and Peter Grazette for their help and long stints without their loved ones; Elly James for her patience; Caroline McArthur and all at Square Peg for their enthusiasm and imagination; Jason Lowe and Joe Woodhouse for the stunning pictures; Smith & Gilmour for their beautiful design; Shirley Patton and Channel 4 Rights for their advice; Clare Barton for her saintly support and Tim Anthill for figuring stuff out; Waheed Alli for his wisdom; Andrew Jackson and Jay Hunt for believing in the idea; Karoline Copping for her clarity and wit; Caroline Ross Pirie, Larissa Hickey, Tim Hancock, Chloe Avery, Lana Salah, Rick Moore, Danny Rorher, Steve Bowden, Toby Everett, Jessica Jones and Jade Hooker for their work across the whole television series, and the entire Alchemy team and crew – I wish I could name you all; Caroline Gove for her special cup cakes; Martha Kearney, Sadie Hennessy, Dee Shulman, Paul Reizin, Miranda Gooch, Sheree Folkson, Susy Hogarth,

Megan Forde, Diane Atkinson, Patrick Wildgust, Judy Gordon Jones, Hilary Townend, Lynette Rees and Tina Jenkins for transforming the blackest pepper into allspice; and special thanks to Charlie Parsons for being a wonderful friend and making it possible.

A special note from Emma: Biggest thank you to my mum who is better than any PA and without whom my contribution would not have been possible; to my family, especially my wonderful son Mateo; Sam Wylde, The Spicery team, Wendy Millyard and the Morris family, who have been so supportive.

A special note from Stevie: I would like to thank my lovely, patient, beautiful wife for always being there and for being an extraordinary mum. To little Sam for not getting too cross with his 'lost' daddy. Also Nicola, for making it all happen. To all the great cooks and hard-working spice growers we have met all over the world, this is really all about you, so thank you for sharing your knowledge so freely. A big thank you to Georgia who did a lot of the hard work. And to Elly for watching my back. Thank you to everyone at Dock Kitchen, particularly Alex and Rich, for always cooking the way I like it.